CRASH COURSE

FIFTEEN WAYS TO BECOME A MORE DEFENSIVE DRIVER

JOSEPH B. FITZGERALD   BENJAMIN R. DAVID

Editing, design, distribution by Bublish

ISBN: 979-8-89989-013-0 (paperback)
ISBN: 979-8-89989-012-3 (eBook)

ABOUT THE AUTHORS

Joe Fitzgerald

 Joe Fitzgerald has dedicated over 25 years to the field of traffic safety, rising through the ranks of the Wilmington Police Department to become a Sergeant in 2010. As a traffic crash reconstructionist, he investigated serious injury and fatal crashes, providing critical insights that often led to expert testimony in various areas including vehicle speed determination, drug and alcohol impaired driving, and standardized field sobriety testing. For over a decade, Joe has run the Southeastern Driver Training Center and has developed a defensive driving curriculum that has spread throughout the country. Joe currently serves as President of the National Crash Prevention Program.

Ben David

Ben David dedicated over 25 years to prosecuting crime, including serving as the elected District Attorney for New Hanover and Pender Counties from 2004 to 2024. During his tenure, Ben oversaw the creation and running of administrative traffic courts, efficiently resolving hundreds of cases in a single court session every week. These courts have been replicated in all 100 counties of North Carolina. He is a certified law enforcement instructor and is an adjunct faculty member at the University of North Carolina Wilmington. He has served as lead trial attorney on several precedent-setting vehicular homicide cases and is a published author and highly sought-after speaker on traffic safety issues. Ben currently serves as Chief Legal Counsel of the National Crash Prevention Program.

CONTENTS

SECTION 1
DISTRACTED DRIVING

SECTION 2
SPEED KILLS

SECTION 3
IMPAIRED DRIVING IS NO ACCIDENT

SECTION 4
MORE DRIVING TIPS TO KEEP YOU SAFE

INTRODUCTION

Statistics in Washington, DC have names in places like Wilmington, NC. We know these stories all too well. Joe put up the crime scene tape for the makeshift memorials on the side of the road. Ben gave the closing arguments for the cases holding people accountable in a courtroom. Since 1999, we have been serving and protecting, giving victims a voice, and speaking for the dead in the cases that have shaped the region and set precedent in our state. After a combined 50 years of responding to these events, we have dedicated ourselves to trying to prevent these tragedies from ever occurring. That is why we wrote this book. One scene we heard about years ago still sticks with us and is a motivating force.

In a peaceful neighborhood, a young man was killed just blocks from his childhood home. His best friend, who had been driving, was grossly impaired on alcohol and crying uncontrollably, cradling his friend's lifeless body when the police arrived. Two officers were assigned to deliver the heartbreaking news to the victim's family, what is called a "death notification." It is the toughest job in law enforcement.

They walked up a crooked path to a beautiful home and caught sight of the family through the bay window, unaware that their lives were about to change forever. There was a mother and father, a young brother, all at a breakfast table, enjoying a meal. The young brother was laughing so hard that food was literally coming out of his mouth. At the table there was also an empty chair, one that would never be filled again.

Just as the more experienced officer raised his hand to knock on the door, the younger officer blurted out: "Wait! Wait, I want to give this family something." The older officer, puzzled, replied, "What on earth could you possibly give this family right now?" The younger officer, with a heavy heart, responded, "Five more minutes. Can we just give them five more minutes before we knock on this door and change their lives forever?" And so, the two officers waited. And then they knocked. The family behind the door was about to hear everyone's worst nightmare and live a "new normal" for the rest of their lives.

We have processed too many crime scenes and have had to meet with too many families at the courthouse. A common refrain from parents in these heartbreaking situations is that they wish their child had called them; they would have come to pick them up without hesitation, no questions asked.

We have taken our message to thousands of young people each year, encouraging them to have honest conversations about choices and consequences before they are given a right to remain silent for some ill-informed decision that they cannot take back. We stress the importance of forming a pact with their parents to reach out for help when they need it. But these driving lessons are not just for the new drivers. They apply to all of us, every time we get behind the wheel.

Police officers and prosecutors often find themselves navigating a dual landscape. On one side, we engage with the public through minor infractions such as speeding or failing to register a vehicle—issues that, while important, rarely define an individual's character. These encounters can serve as a reminder that if these are the gravest transgressions one faces, life has been relatively fortunate. However, the other side of this reality presents a stark contrast: serious crimes like murder, burglary, and drug trafficking that inflict profound harm on communities. These are the cases that inspired many to join the force or pursue a career in law. The challenge lies in prioritizing these severe offenses without losing sight of the minor ones: if everything is treated as a priority, then nothing truly is.

To address this, we started an administrative traffic court in Wilmington, a groundbreaking approach that has since gained recognition as a best practice across North Carolina and beyond. We discovered that 99% of individuals cited for traffic violations were not interested in contesting their tickets; rather, they sought to avoid the repercussions that could affect their insurance and driving records. This insight led us to streamline the process, without the need for a judge or police presence in the courtroom, by sending people to driving school in exchange for a dismissal or plea to a non-moving violation.

We also recognized the importance of transforming the educational aspect of traffic school into a more engaging experience. To achieve this, we developed an online driving school that complements this book, integrating the lessons learned from our interactions on the streets and in the courtroom. By doing so, we aim to provide a comprehensive resource that is both informative and entertaining, fostering a deeper understanding of road safety and the law among drivers.

We combine statistics, science, and stories, to impart the three keys to decision-making and the fifteen driving tips that are in this book to becoming a more defensive driver. Each month, hundreds of people log onto our website, nationalcpp.org (The National Crash Prevention Program) to watch us cover this material and interview families, first responders, and others who have been directly or indirectly affected by some of the biggest cases we have handled.

Maybe you were required to watch that video series, either the four-hour version or eight-hour version, after being directed by a prosecutor or judge in response to receiving a traffic ticket. Maybe someone sent you the link. Maybe you were handed this book and are learning about the video series for the first time. Regardless, this book and companion video series is our attempt to prevent one more family receiving a knock on the door. We hope to create a safer future for everyone by sharing what we have learned along the way. Simply put, we are tired of responding to tragedies and we want to prevent them.

STOPPING THE FATAL THREE

Each year the U.S. averages between 30,000 and 40,000 deaths on our roadways. Joe served in many roles as an officer, including on the SWAT team. Ben tried the most violent offenders in the system for a quarter of a century as a prosecutor. Both of us agree: The deadliest weapon in America is not a gun or a knife or the hands and feet of an abusive spouse – it is a car; a car that is being driven by someone who is speeding, distracted, and/ or impaired.

Nearly all these deaths are preventable and are caused by human error. We cannot tell you where the next bank robbery is going to happen. It is impossible to stop all crime. But most of the carnage we see on the roads is entirely preventable and comes down to good people making bad choices.

It is important to have a complete understanding of what behaviors are causing the most deaths on our roadways. First, imagine there is a deadly disaster or event approaching our country that would result in the death of nearly 20,000 people. However, we can avoid this tragic event by simply pushing a button. Would you press the button? Of course you would. Distracted driving, speeding, and impaired driving account for nearly 60% of the deaths on our roads each year. That's more than 55 people every day who lose their lives because of another individual's poor choices. These are individuals who decide to text or use social media while they drive, ignore the speed limit and drive recklessly, or decide to get behind the wheel after drinking or consuming some type of impairing substance. Each of these actions started with a choice.

It seems like the overall attitude towards motor vehicle deaths in our country is a little on the apathetic side. Motor vehicle deaths are looked upon by many with a "cost of doing business" attitude. It is easy to have that attitude if your life has never been impacted by the loss of a loved one due to a motor vehicle crash. When it does happen, and for many reading this book there's a good chance at some point you will experience the loss of a loved one due to a motor vehicle crash, you will reflect upon the circumstances and think how easily the crash that took your loved one could have been avoided if only someone had made a better decision.

What if every driver made the decision to avoid these three behaviors? What if everyone made the choice to put their phone down while driving? What if everyone decided to drive the speed limit and not get behind the wheel if they've been consuming an impairing substance? We would have more than 20,000 people making it home to their families every year. The reality is that we all have the power to save lives if we choose to make responsible decisions when we get behind the wheel.

THREE KEYS TO MAKING SUCCESSFUL DECISIONS

Driving while you are distracted, intentionally speeding, and getting behind the wheel after you have consumed drugs and alcohol all involve choices. What makes a person a safe driver? It is not only their ability to handle and control a vehicle. It's not only their experience. It's these things plus their ability to make good decisions. After careers spent handling every type of case under the sun and trying to make sense of the wreckage that comes from poor decisions, we have distilled these life lessons into three key points, or guide posts for making good choices: 1) Know your purpose, 2) Surround yourself with the right people, and 3) Every decision comes with a consequence. These lessons are not only based upon common sense, but they are also backed by legal principles that have real world applications. We will be diving into these three key points one at a time over the next three sections of this book.

CRIME AND PUNISHMENT

How defendants are punished, and whether they are even punished at all, comes down to the labels the law affixes to their conduct. Labels have meaning. Most people have heard: "The punishment should fit the crime." The critical questions to ask when a tragedy occurs are: 1) Is this a crime at all, and 2) If it is a crime, what do we call it?

Every loss is a tragedy. But whether that conduct is punished, and the degree of punishment involved, depends upon how the conduct is labeled. Most states, including North Carolina, have structured sentencing. This means that a certain punishment level follows a plea or conviction for misdemeanors and felonies according to how they are classified. Imagine walking up a ladder of guilt, from the bottom rung to the top:

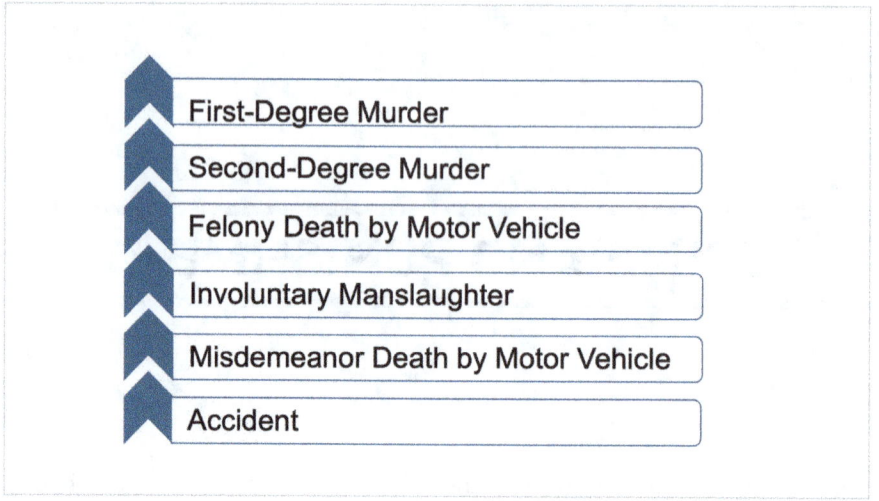

Accident: There may still be civil liability for negligence, exposing the defendant to massive monetary damages, but there are no criminal penalties.

Misdemeanor Death by Motor Vehicle: This is a traffic collision where criminal negligence is involved, such as running a red light. First-time offenders face the potential of limited jail time or no more than 150 days and most get a probationary sentence.

Involuntary Manslaughter: This is when someone acts in a culpably negligent manner, when fatal consequences are foreseeable, such as violating a safety statute like texting and driving. First-time offenders can be sentenced to probation or face incarceration for around 1-2 years.

Felony Death by Motor Vehicle: This is a traffic fatality committed by someone who is impaired by drugs and alcohol. Even for a person with no prior record, the punishment is usually around 5 years in prison, a substantial increase given the great work of M.A.D.D and other organizations.

Second-Degree Murder: Killing with malice. This means not only a killing done with hatred, ill will, or spite (this is actual malice), but where malice is implied from the circumstances. These are cases where there is a conscious disregard for the rights and safety of others, or when a person is deliberately bent on mischief. This can include drag racing, fleeing to elude police officers, and impaired driving offenses where someone has a prior conviction for DWI. Punishment for first-time offenders ranges from approximately 8 to 21 years for these offenses.

First-Degree Murder: Killing with premeditation and deliberation OR felony murder (killing in the perpetration of another violent felony like armed robbery). This can include when someone intentionally uses the car as a deadly weapon and drives into a crowd (like the acts of terror that have become all too common) or when someone kills someone in a car while committing another violent felony, such as fleeing from a bank robbery. The mandatory minimum punishment for first-degree murder is life in prison without parole. Some states, including North Carolina, also have the death penalty.

Ultimately, ascending the ladder of guilt involves examining the guilty mind ("Mens Rae" in Latin) of the defendant, which runs along a continuum from negligence to recklessness to malice, and finally, to premeditation and deliberation. As we explore the many case studies in this book, it will become clear that while the circumstances may lead to the same tragic outcome, the thought processes of the defendant, and especially his or her prior behavior, can result in vastly different punishments.

FIFTEEN TIPS FOR BECOMING A MORE DEFENSIVE DRIVER

Everyone with a driver's license can become a defensive driver. It's just a matter of whether we will make that choice. In the four sections that follow, we are going to cover driving tips. Done consistently, they will become habits. Just as bad habits can be deadly, good habits keep you alive. As the Greek philosopher Aristotle said more than 2,400 years ago: "We are what we repeatedly do. Excellence then is not an act, but a habit." Here are the 15 tips we will cover in this book:

1) Avoid Distractions: Manual, visual and cognitive.

2) Maintain Situational Awareness: Know what's going on around you.

3) Watch Your Speed: More speed = less time to react.

4) Avoid Impaired Driving: Drugs and alcohol, even in low amounts, can impact your ability to drive. Plan ahead so you don't get behind the wheel and take the keys away from friends.

5) Wear Your Seatbelt: Give yourself every advantage to avoid possible injury or death.

6) Avoid Unprotected Left Turns Across Busy Streets: Don't take unnecessary risks. Take a safer, less risky route even if it takes a few extra minutes. When in doubt, wait.

7) Handling Tailgaters: Build in reaction time between you and the vehicle in front of you. Don't brake check the tailgater.

8) Avoiding Head-On Collisions: Think ahead in case you are confronted by a vehicle traveling the wrong direction in your lane.

9) Know Your Location: Always know your location in the event an emergency arises, and you need to call for help.

10) Maintain Your Vehicle: Don't drive an unsafe vehicle; keep it in good working order.

11) Plan Your Route: Know in advance which lanes to be in and which lanes to avoid.

12) Avoid Road Rage Situations: Let it go. Nothing good can come from lashing out.

13) Protect Yourself Financially: Take appropriate steps to protect yourself and your family.

14) Don't Drive in Another Vehicle's Blind Spot: Do not assume another driver sees you. If people are not using a turn signal, they are probably not checking their blind spots either.

15) Expect Others to Make Mistakes: That's the whole premise of this book. By expecting these mistakes, we stay alert and are more attentive.

If you follow the three keys to successful decision-making and the 15 tips that we have listed above every time you get behind the wheel, then you will undoubtedly be one of the most defensive drivers on the road. But again, you must choose to follow this advice as well as the rules of the road. We owe it to our friends and families to do everything in our power to make it back home each time we head out and onto the road. We owe it to the other families we share the road with too.

SECTION 1

DISTRACTED DRIVING

According to the National Highway Traffic Safety Administration (NHTSA), more than 3,000 people are killed each year by a distracted driver.[1] These numbers are surely an underestimate because in many cases it is impossible for investigating officers to determine if distraction was a factor in the fatality. There are three types of distractions: 1) Visual distractions take your eyes from the road; 2) Manual distractions take at least one hand from the steering wheel; 3) Cognitive distractions take your mind off the task of driving.

---

[1] National Highway Traffic Safety Administration. (n.d.). *Distracted driving.* U.S. Department of Transportation. https://www.nhtsa.gov/risky-driving/distracted-driving Accessed 2/22/2025

TIP #1: AVOID DISTRACTIONS

Most people immediately think of texting and driving when we talk about distracted driving. The reality is much bigger than texting and includes using the phone for social media, shuffling playlists, setting GPS apps, and eating. Our longtime colleague Mark Anderson, a crash investigator with the Wilmington Police Department, likes to lay out this scenario. Would you get in the ring with Mike Tyson? Most of you would say no. He could hurt or even kill you. Some might like the thrill of the challenge and say yes. But there is a catch: you must hold a phone in your dominant hand and use it during the entire match. How do you like your chances now? Driving is even more deadly and yet many of us think nothing of tying up our best hand when driving directly at cars that give us less reaction time than one of Iron Mike's punches.

There is another distraction that is often overlooked: other people in your car. According to AAA studies, when young drivers add other young passengers to their vehicle the likelihood of them becoming involved in a fatal crash significantly rises.[2] Many states have laws that limit the number of passengers that a young person can have in their car for the first few months they have a driver's license.

---

[2] AAA Exchange: Teen Driver Distraction. Available at https://exchange.aaa.com/teen-driver-distraction/#.XoeIiYOSk2w. Accessed on 4/3/2020.

Here's the question: if we know how dangerous distracted driving is, why do we still engage in the distracted behaviors? Because we simply never think it's going to happen to us. And if we engage in the behavior and get away with it, we are emboldened to do it again. This pattern works until it doesn't.

The first time someone sends a text message while they are driving, they are probably thinking to themselves "I better be careful." After they do it once without any kind of negative consequence, they gradually build their confidence in texting while driving and begin to think that they can do it safely. It's important to remember that it only takes one bad day, one bad decision to change or end someone's life.

We often get asked if it's safer to talk on the phone while driving using a Bluetooth device versus holding your phone to your ear. The research indicates that it's not any safer using a Bluetooth device. Why? Because it's not the act of holding your phone to your ear that's the distraction, it is the conversation.

Three cases involving distracted driving stand out for us. In the first case, a young woman named Alexandra was riding on a motorcycle and was struck by a man who was merely looking at his phone. He was not even texting or making a call. Alexandra was very seriously injured in the crash. She ended up having to have her left arm and left leg amputated. She is no longer able to dance, an activity she loves, and has a hard time cooking for her children. Alexandra has not lost her voice and now helps use it to spread the message about the harmful impacts that distracted driving can have on everyone.

In another case, a young woman ran a red light late one night and collided with a Toyota Camry carrying three young women in their twenties, killing one of them. The young woman who caused the crash admitted to Joe to being on her cell phone talking to her boyfriend. Even though it was at night with very little traffic, she didn't see the bright red light in front of her because her mind was somewhere else. She was cognitively distracted and failed to process the information necessary for safe driving. Not only was she convicted of a serious felony, but she had to live with the knowledge that she took a completely innocent person's life and seriously injured two others.

In a third case, Joe investigated a man who rolled his Ford Expedition while reaching down to retrieve a piece of fried chicken he had just purchased. The distraction caused his vehicle to drift off the roadway, forcing him to quickly jerk the wheel back to the left when he realized his error. This overcorrection caused his vehicle to rotate and overturn. He was ejected from the Expedition and died when he impacted the roadway.

Driving is what we consider a "divided attention task." Meaning, when you're driving, you're doing several small tasks simultaneously. The more additional and unnecessary tasks we add to driving, the more difficult and riskier it becomes. No one is immune from this, no matter their level of experience. Even highly trained police officers can get distracted.

Joe remembers one night as a police officer when he responded to a non-emergency noise violation call. It was around 10:00 p.m. on a weekday night and fortunately traffic wasn't very heavy. As he was driving, he glanced down at his MDT (mobile data terminal – car computer) to get further directions regarding the location of this call. Glancing down at the computer caused him to take his eyes off the road for only a moment, but it distracted him from realizing that the traffic light ahead was red. There was no time to stop the vehicle. Fortunately, the other drivers waiting to cross the intersection with a green light were doing exactly what they were supposed to be doing and noticed that Joe wasn't slowing down for the red light. They just sat and watched as a marked police car ran through a solid red light.

Joe was extremely embarrassed and grateful that he didn't crash into someone else. Some of you may be wondering, did he write himself a ticket for the red light violation? The answer is no, but he did let another driver off with a warning for a red light violation later that night. None of us are immune to the consequences if we are driving while distracted.

At the end of the day the solution to the distracted driving problem is very simple. When you're driving, just drive. This is such an important point that we will highlight a similar concept in Tip #2, maintain situational awareness. Unfortunately, in our technologically connected world it becomes very hard to do anything without being sidetracked by a notification of some type. Phone calls, text messages, emails, etc. We are receiving notifications throughout the day that keep our minds and bodies busy and constantly working.

Here are some tips to help us avoid driving while distracted:

1. Put your phone away. "Out of sight, out of mind." If we place our phones in view where we can see or hear the notifications, it becomes extremely tempting to check those notifications even when we're driving. To avoid this, put your phone in your glovebox or center console.

2. Utilize "driving mode." Most mobile phone carriers now offer a feature designed to eliminate distractions while driving. Selecting this option while driving will reduce distractions, and most will send a notification to those trying to reach you indicating that you are driving.

3. Think about the big picture. No task we complete on our phone is worth injuring or taking another's life. Remember that it only takes one lapse in judgment to become involved in a life-changing crash.

4. Parents must set an example. If parents don't want their child to text and drive, then they shouldn't text and drive. For two decades Ben spoke to every 8th grade class and 12th grade class

in his District about driving safety. He would ask students if, as a much younger child, they remembered looking at their mother, father, grandparent, or babysitter, and seeing them using the phone to text and drive. All the student's hands would shoot into the air. We cannot say one thing and do another and expect our children to act responsibly. For our driver's education classes for new drivers, students are with a driving instructor in a classroom for 30 hours and an additional six hours in a car. They have ridden with a parent their entire life. Who do you think has the greater influence on that new driver?

Avoiding distractions is an ongoing battle that every driver fights each time they get behind the wheel. Whether it's with their phone, their passengers, roadside objects/events, or even their own mind. Distractions are everywhere. But at the end of the day, like all other decisions, it comes down to a choice we make. Drivers must be intentional about avoiding and refraining from distractions. We also must avoid becoming overconfident in our own abilities and understand that no matter how great of a driver we think we are, anyone can crash when they become distracted. Defensive drivers are not distracted drivers.

TIP #2: MAINTAIN SITUATIONAL AWARENESS

Any time you're driving down the road you need to know what's going on around you. We call this situational awareness. You need to know what's going on in front of you, what's happening beside you, and even what's happening behind you. By having a full understanding of what's going on around you and your vehicle, you will make better decisions more quickly. To help develop and maintain situational awareness we must adopt a tactical mindset, which essentially means we are always looking out for potential threats and hazards and thinking ahead. One of the ways we can do this while driving is by utilizing the Smith System.

The Smith System was developed in 1952 by a man named Harold Smith and consists of five rules designed to help drivers identify potential hazards as early as possible and then appropriately handle those hazards. Here's a breakdown of the five rules:

Rule #1 of the Smith System: Aim High in Steering. When driving down the road, a driver should look ahead to where their vehicle will be within the next 10–15 seconds. By doing this, they can identify potential hazards early on. When a driver identifies potential hazards early, this gives them more time to formulate a plan to deal with the hazard. The more time a driver has to plan, the better their plan will be.

When it comes to driving, time is equal to distance. At 60 mph a vehicle is traveling 88 feet each second. If the driver of that vehicle identifies a car pulling out in front of them 10 seconds ahead, they have 880 feet to begin slowing to avoid a crash. Identify potential hazards as early as possible.

Rule #2 of the Smith System: Get the Big Picture. When driving you want to collect as much information as possible to help recognize and identify any potential threats. For example, if you're walking through the woods you wouldn't expect to be run over by a city bus but rather you would be alert for threats that are common to that environment, like snakes and bears. When driving, if you see yellow pentagon-shaped signs you should immediately begin thinking about the potential hazards associated with schools: kids playing, crossing guards, school buses, and parents picking up or dropping off their children. Same for construction zones: orange signs mean you should begin thinking about workers nearby, heavy machinery entering the roadway, or debris that might be on the road. Getting the big picture means you understand what the potential threats could be based upon the available information.

Rule #3 of the Smith System: Keep Your Eyes Moving. When drivers stare straight ahead it becomes very easy to "zone-out." However, when we keep our eyes moving, we are constantly taking in new information that keeps our minds engaged in the driving task and makes us able to detect potential threats approaching from our peripheral vision. Any time you are approaching an intersection you should begin scanning the intersection before you begin crossing through it. You should be watching for other vehicles approaching the intersection that don't appear to be slowing for their red light. Also watching for cyclists and pedestrians crossing the intersection. As you continue to travel through the intersection, continue to scan to your left, right, and ahead.

Anytime you are stopped at a red light, especially when you are the first car in line, make sure to scan to your left and right before entering the intersection. Most red light violations occur within 1-2 seconds of the light changing. This would mean the car they collide with is usually the first car in line when their light changes to green. That doesn't mean you can let your guard down if you're not the first car. It just means you should be especially cautious when you are in that position. Also, keep your eyes moving when you're driving and especially as you're traveling through intersections.

Rule #4 of the Smith System: Leave Yourself an Out. One aspect of situational awareness is always having an escape route in the event an emergency arises. There are two techniques that drivers can employ to ensure they are leaving themselves a way out.

1) Maintain a safe following distance. What is a safe following distance? Years ago, drivers went by a rule stating you should have one car length of following distance per 10 miles per hour. So, at 50mph you should have five car lengths of following distance according to this rule. The problem with this rule is that most drivers aren't sure what distance is considered a car length. Is it the length of a Prius (about 15') or is it the length of a Chevy Suburban (about 18')? Even if we said a car length is 10 feet, how well do you think most drivers will do estimating 50 feet while traveling 50 mph down the road?

It's for those reasons that we now utilize a different method based upon how many seconds we are behind another vehicle. We call this method the Three Second Rule. Essentially it states when the vehicle ahead passes a stationary landmark (roadway marking, shadow, sign, etc.) it should take you at least three seconds, under ideal conditions, before you reach that same landmark. For example, when the car in front of you passes the white stop line at an intersection you would begin counting 1001, 1002, 1003 until you reach the same stop line. If you count to 1003, then you're three seconds behind that vehicle. For every hazardous condition you add one second of following distance. If it's raining, instead of maintaining three seconds of following distance you would want to increase your following distance to at least four seconds. If it's raining and dark out, then you would increase your following distance to at least five seconds.

A very high percentage of the crashes in urban areas are rear-end collisions. Your attention and following distance are your number one defense against rear end collisions. How so? Maintaining adequate following distance not only reduces the likelihood of crashing into the car ahead but also allows for smoother stops, decreasing the chances of being hit from behind.

2)   When you stop behind another vehicle make sure you can see that vehicle's rear tires touching the pavement.

If you can see the rear tires of the vehicle stopped ahead of you this ensures you have room to turn out from behind this car if it breaks down in the roadway or an emergency arises. If you are too close to the vehicle in front of you, that doesn't allow room to turn out without striking the rear bumper of the vehicle ahead unless you back up first. It can be very challenging to back up if traffic is heavy.

Using the picture above, if we are stopped and happen to spot a vehicle approaching us from behind and the driver doesn't appear to be slowing down, we have enough room to pull to the right in hopes of avoiding being struck from behind by the inattentive driver.

Defensive drivers always try to leave themselves an out and are on the lookout for other drivers who might not be paying attention or driving carelessly. Make it a habit when you're stopped to glance into your rearview mirror to see what traffic behind you is doing.

Rule #5 of the Smith System: *Make Sure They See You.* Making sure others can see you is simply understanding that there are things drivers can do to make themselves more visible. One thing drivers can do to make themselves more visible is use their headlights. This is why most newer model cars come equipped with daytime running lights. They make you more visible, especially in inclement weather or any time visibility is reduced. Other examples include using your horn when you need to warn someone you are approaching or using your turn signals when you are approaching your turn or changing lanes. Many people on our roads have grown accustomed to not using their turn signals, but it is a simple way to get the attention of those around you. Defensive drivers do not cut corners. They do everything possible to make sure they are visible to others and use every advantage available to lessen the likelihood of becoming involved in a crash.

It is also worth noting that the color of your vehicle affects visibility. Have you ever wondered why many state's highway patrol vehicles are silver in color? Silver and gray cars tend to blend in with the roadway or sky in the background and appear camouflaged. This helps law enforcement to be more effective at traffic enforcement. The same is true of our military. What color tanks and equipment do you find our military using in the Middle East? Sand-colored equipment because it blends in with the environment. If you're driving a gray or silver vehicle you may be making yourself less visible to other motorists. We are not suggesting that you need to immediately go out and sell the brand-new gray car you bought, but you might want to make sure that you are always using your headlights.

If you follow the rules of the Smith System, it helps to ensure that you maintain situational awareness and always know what's going on around you. As a defensive driver you always need a good understanding of your circumstances if you want to make the best possible decision in an emergency. Crashes happen very quickly and to avoid a crash, you must stay alert and watchful.

KEY #1: KNOW YOUR PURPOSE

Closely associated with situational awareness and avoiding distractions is reminding yourself that you have a purpose when you drive. Most immediately, it means that when you get behind the wheel your reason for driving, your sole focus, should be getting from point A to point B as efficiently and safely as possible. But reminding yourself that you have a purpose goes even deeper than that.

Take a moment and look around you. What do you see? Maybe you see a television, sofa, chairs, lamps, picture frames, a clock, and several other items of room décor. Each one of these items was made by someone. The person that made these items made them with the thought that they would make someone's life a little better. When they were created, they were created with a purpose in mind.

This book was created with a purpose in mind. Regardless of your spiritual beliefs you must believe that you were created by something. Either you were created by an act of science or by a divine being. Either way, the conclusion is the same. You were CREATED, and anything that is created is created with a purpose in mind. This is important because when you realize that you have a great purpose, you are more likely to make decisions that will help and protect this purpose.

In his famous speech *Acres of Diamonds*, Russell Conwell shares a story he learned in 1870 while traveling along the Tigris River with a Turkish guide. The story follows a Persian man named Ali Hafed, who lived a comfortable life on a prosperous farm, providing well for his family. One day, a visiting priest spoke to Ali about diamonds, describing their immense value and claiming that with just a handful, one could achieve great wealth and power—enough to place one's children on thrones.

That conversation planted a seed of discontent in Ali's mind. That night, though nothing in his life had changed, he went to bed feeling poor. The next morning, driven by a growing obsession with finding diamonds, he sold his farm and set out on a quest to find them. His journey took him across distant lands—Palestine, Europe, and eventually Spain—but no matter where he looked, diamonds remained elusive. In time, his fortune disappeared, and despair consumed him. In a moment of hopelessness, Ali ended his own life, drowning in the waves of the sea.

But the story does not end there. Back at Ali's former farm, the new owner led his camel to a nearby brook. As the animal drank, the man noticed something unusual—a bright flash from a stone in the water. Curious, he picked it up and brought it inside, placing it on his mantle.

Sometime later, the same priest who had once spoken to Ali visited the farm. Upon seeing the stone, he was astonished. "This is a diamond!" he declared. The new owner, skeptical, replied, "That's just a rock from my garden." But the priest was certain. They went to the brook and discovered more of these shining stones. It turned out that Ali's farm was sitting on what would become the Golconda diamond mines—one of the richest diamond sources in history.

Ali had spent his life searching for wealth in distant lands, unaware that the treasure he longed for had been beneath his feet all along. How often do people do the same—chasing opportunity elsewhere without recognizing the potential right in front of them? Understanding our own purpose and the resources around us is crucial; otherwise, we risk making poor choices, not realizing the value of what we already have.

We recall a case where four high school students died in a high-speed car crash. These four young people were sitting on so much purpose and opportunity but one poor decision, to drive at an extreme speed, cost them everything. A short-sighted "YOLO" (You Only Live Once) mindset can be a purpose-killer. This can be applied to many things: the first time a person decides to experiment with drugs; the decision of a married person to have an affair; the decision to drive home after having too many alcoholic drinks. Those are all short-sighted decisions that can destroy a person's purpose.

Teenagers and young adults are especially susceptible to making rash decisions. According to an article published by the American Academy of Child & Adolescent Psychiatry, the portion of the brain that controls a person's reasoning is not fully developed until well into adulthood. As a result, we often see teens and young adults making impulsive, high-risk decisions that result in tragic consequences.[3] It is no wonder that the insurance rates for young drivers are much higher than the rates for more mature drivers.

A person who makes good decisions can look at a given situation or dilemma and ask themselves, "Does the decision I'm about to make have the potential to take me closer or further away from my purpose?" If everyone took a moment to ask themselves this one question, we would see people making much better decisions and our roads would be much safer.

---

[3] American Academy of Child and Adolescent Psychiatry. (n.d.). The Teen Brain: Behavior, Problem Solving, and Decision Making. Retrieved from https://www.aacap.org/AACAP/Families_and_Youth/Facts_for_Families/FFF-Guide/The-Teen-Brain-Behavior-Problem-Solving-and-Decision-Making-095.aspx

SECTION 2

SPEED KILLS

If you are about to become involved in a crash, what's the one thing you wish you had? More time. Time gives you the ability to better process information, make better decisions and execute those decisions. How do you get more time? You slow down. The faster you travel the less time you have to identify and react to potential hazards that appear. Not to mention, the faster you're traveling the more severe the impact will be if you strike another object.

According to NHTSA (National Highway Traffic Safety Administration), nearly one third of all U.S. traffic deaths were attributed to speed. That equates to nearly 12,000 lives.[4] Often many drivers seem to forget

---

[4] National Highway Traffic Safety Administration. (2023, July 19). *Speeding-related fatalities reach 14-year high*. U.S. Department of Transportation. https://www.nhtsa. gov/press-releases/speed-campaign-speeding-fatalities-14-year-high. Accessed 2/22/ 2025

that when speed limits are established, they aren't just numbers decided at random, they are set to safe speeds based upon roadway surface type, curvature of the roadway, and other environmental factors such as the presence of homes and businesses.

TIP #3: WATCH YOUR SPEED

Before we go any further, let's look at a few interesting facts on speeding provided by the Insurance Institute for Highway Safety:[5]

- Males are more likely than females to exceed the posted speed limit.
- As speed limits increase so do the number of fatalities.
- Speed increases the crash energy exponentially. For example, when impact speed increases from 40 to 60 mph (a 50% increase), the energy that needs to be managed increases by 125%.

Speeding becomes especially dangerous at night. On average a vehicle's high beam headlights will illuminate anywhere from 350' to 500' ahead. If a car is traveling 90 mph it is covering roughly 132 feet each second. So, the driver could cover the distance lit by their headlights in approximately 2.5 seconds, depending on the condition of the headlights. Let's say, as the driver is speeding down the roadway, he sees an object in the middle of the road. He must immediately decide how to address the object (steer away or brake). Once he decides what action to take, he must react and make it happen. Let's say this driver has a reaction time of .75 seconds. Considering

---

[5] Speed. Available at: https://www.iihs.org/topics/speed#overview. Accessed 1/18/2020

reaction time, the original 2.5 seconds has now decreased to 1.75 seconds. Unfortunately, with this little amount of time many drivers make incorrect decisions that often lead to crashes. The higher the speed the less time there is available to make these life and death decisions. Ultimately, the faster we are traveling the more likely we are to die in a traffic crash.

What makes speeding deaths so tragic is that they are easily prevented. By simply letting off the accelerator we can increase the likelihood that we and other motorists will make it home safely. So many of these speeding deaths occur when young people (usually males) get caught up living in the moment when things are seemingly perfect in their life and nothing can go wrong. Studies suggest that the largest number of speeding deaths occur on the weekends.[6] You can almost visualize the scenario: a couple of teenagers hanging out for the day and riding around town, windows down and music up. Everything seems perfect in their world so the driver presses down on the accelerator a little more than normal thinking nothing can go wrong, until it does. Perhaps sometimes it's good to live in the moment, but when it's done irresponsibly it can have disastrous consequences.

Our culture has a way of glamorizing risky behaviors such as reckless driving through fictional action movies. Teenagers will watch these movies and become inspired by what they see and attempt to replicate the driving behaviors they see. As we know, things don't always end like they do in the movies and in real life it costs lives.

What would your answer be if we asked you how fast you normally drive in a 60 mph speed zone? Many seem to believe that you are safe if you don't go more than 10 mph over the speed limit. Even a few miles per hour can make a big difference. For example, let's assume you're driving on

---

6   National Highway Traffic Safety Administration. (2023, May). *Overview of motor vehicle crashes in 2021* (Report No. DOT HS 813 473). U.S. Department of Transportation. https://crashstats.nhtsa.dot.gov/Api/Public/ViewPublication/813473.pdf   Accessed 2/22/2025

---

a road with a speed limit of 60 mph and that's the speed you're driving. You notice a hazard appearing 250 feet ahead. If it were a hazard that requires you to come to a stop it would take between 230 feet and 250 feet to accomplish this task. At 60 mph you would hopefully be able to stop before striking the hazard 250 feet away. Now let's say instead of going the speed limit you're traveling at 70 mph when you see the hazard 250 feet away. Could you stop? Considering reaction time and braking distance it would take more than 300 feet to come to a stop, after striking the hazard. A few miles per hour faster can make a big difference in terms of whether you can stop and the force of the impact.

Here are a few suggestions to help avoid speeding:

1) Leave early. This will reduce the need and desire to exceed the speed limit to make it to your destination. This also leaves time if you encounter unexpected delays. Never leave just in time to make it to your destination. Plan to arrive a few minutes early.

2) Remember the big picture. Don't get caught up in the moment or thrill of speeding. Instead remember that it only takes one crash to completely change everything and end someone's life.

3) Speeding doesn't really save that much time. In towns riddled with stop lights and traffic, speeding usually doesn't even save much time. In fact, it's more likely to slow you down in the event you're stopped by law enforcement or become involved in a crash. For example, let's say you're traveling to a town that's 70 miles away and you're driving the speed limit which is 70 mph. How long will it take to reach your destination? That's right, one hour. Now let's say you're in a hurry and you're driving 90 mph in the 70 mph speed zone. How much time would you save? Roughly 14 minutes. However, there's a good chance that going that speed you will get stopped by law enforcement. The average traffic stop

takes approximately 15 minutes. The stop alone will take you more time than you tried to save by speeding. Not to mention, now you have a court date and will probably be mandated to take a defensive driving class. You would have been much better off just driving the speed limit.

Defensive drivers know and understand that speed reduces the time they have to respond in emergency situations and avoid taking unnecessary risks.

MURDER FROM TWO MILES AWAY

Police officers are sworn to protect and serve the public. Their jobs are both difficult and dangerous. Every time they clock in, they put their lives on the line. When putting on that uniform, they have a duty to act.

When these officers lose their lives in the line of duty, there is no higher priority case in the criminal justice system. In the last three decades, only one officer has been killed by a suspect in our hometown. We were the two people called upon to investigate the crash and prosecute the case in a courtroom.

In the early morning hours of February 18, 2009, Corporal Will Richards, an experienced vice and narcotics detective, drove a patrol car through a quiet neighborhood. Corporal Richards was widely respected on the force. When he spoke, other officers listened. On this night, he was acting supervisor in charge of B-Platoon and was in radio communication with Officer Rich Matthews.

At approximately 1:15 a.m., Corporal Richards observed a GMC Yukon that he believed matched the description of an SUV that had been involved in a kidnapping incident the night before. He followed the vehicle, searching for suspicious activity. The Yukon initially stopped in a business parking lot and appeared to be hiding. Soon after, it exited the parking lot and began speeding. Corporal Richards turned on his blue lights, which simultaneously started a video recording device in the car. The ensuing pursuit was caught on video.

When Corporal Richards activated the emergency equipment, the Yukon initially pulled over. It remained parked for a few seconds. As Corporal Richards attempted to exit his vehicle, the car took off unexpectedly. Corporal Richards gave chase. During the pursuit, the Yukon reached speeds of 65 mph in a 25-mph-zone, sped through three stop signs without slowing down, crossed into the oncoming traffic lane several times, and swerved off and on the road. Five one-pound bags of marijuana were thrown from the vehicle at various points along the chase route.

Given Corporal Richards' extensive experience with narcotics, he immediately recognized the substance being thrown from the car and understood by the volume of drugs what caliber of dealers he was chasing. During the pursuit, Corporal Richards stated, "I need somebody" over the radio, requesting assistance from other officers. He also identified the bags and their locations. Officers around the city were listening.

Officer Matthews and partner Officer Allison Jahreis, both with the B-Platoon, were parked next to each other several miles away. Both turned on their blue lights and sirens and drove toward where the chase was occurring. The in-car cameras from both assisting officers' vehicles show their route of travel and their manner of driving. Traffic was light in those early morning hours, the weather conditions were perfect, and the road, Shipyard Boulevard, was almost entirely straight.

Officer Matthews was in the lead with Officer Jahreis following. Matthews encountered three intersections with traffic lights during the pursuit. Between the lights, he traveled at high rates of speed, reaching up to 105 mph at one point. At all intersections with red lights, Officer Matthews slowed to a near stop, making sure that it was clear before proceeding through. Officer Jahreis followed Officer Matthews at a distance of nine seconds, closing in to four seconds since she did not encounter red lights.

As Officer Matthews reached a top speed of 105 mph, a cardboard box (which was later determined to be empty) suddenly came into view in the middle of the road. He instinctively jerked the steering wheel to the left, a move that proved fatal. The back end of the vehicle (which had recently been serviced and was working properly) slid out and the car bolted across the median. At this point, the feed for the in-car camera was lost. Officer Matthews' vehicle continued to the other side of the road and struck a stand of trees. Officer Jahreis pulled off the road, called for backup and medical assistance, and began attempts to help Officer Matthews. It was no use. Officer Matthews was dead within seconds of impact.

Officer Matthews wrecked just 0.6 miles from the location from which the defendants first fled. Records from the WPD establish that Corporal Richards' chase was still active when Officer Matthews wrecked and did not end until 20 seconds afterward, when the driver of the Yukon finally pulled over. Corporal Richards was able to stop the vehicle without the assistance of the other pursuing officers.

Inside were three people: Anthony (the driver), Eric (front seat passenger), and Matthew (in the back). Later, investigators determined that the three men had robbed other drug dealers of the five pounds of marijuana mere minutes before being stopped by Corporal Richards. The other drug dealers, who were also armed, chased Anthony, Eric, and Matthew after they took off with their drugs. In essence, one chase turned into another. The three men were outrunning other criminals from a lucrative and very dangerous robbery when Corporal Richards first attempted to stop them.

Along the chase route, officers located all five bags of marijuana. Together the drugs had a street value of approximately $30,000. A 40 caliber Glock handgun, loaded with multiple rounds of hollow-point bullets, was also found.

None of the three defendants were strangers to law enforcement. In fact, all had extensive felony records meaning that all were prohibited from possessing the loaded firearm that was later recovered. Additionally, all were either on probation or parole and faced a return to prison if apprehended. It was now time to seek maximum justice.

ACTING IN CONCERT

When two or more people join forces to commit a crime, each can be held responsible for each other's actions. For example, the getaway driver is just as guilty as the person who goes inside the store with a gun and ski mask. Both can be charged with armed robbery since they are working together with the intent to do the crime.

While it is true that there was only one driver who stepped on the gas and started the police chase, the other two passengers were far from innocent. They were complicit in the risks that were created that fateful night. They were felons who had joined forces to rob other drug dealers at gunpoint, with the intention to re-sell the marijuana in our community. Eric was on federal probation, having been released from prison after serving a two-year sentence for transporting drugs and firearms across the Canadian border. He had arrest warrants related to drug and driving offenses from two different counties in North Carolina.

Like Eric, Matthew also had multiple prior contacts with the law, including convictions for drug trafficking. Just a week earlier he had pled guilty to felony fleeing to elude arrest just up the road in Johnston County. At the time of that arrest, $181,000 was seized from his vehicle and another $10,000 was found in his wallet.

Given their lengthy records and the severity of the case, we worked with federal prosecutors to seek maximum justice. Federal sentencing laws for drugs, especially where firearms are involved, are much harsher than in state court. Matthew ultimately went to prison for nearly 12 years for possession of a firearm in furtherance of a drug trafficking crime. Eric received a 13-year sentence for federal conspiracy to possess with the intent to distribute more than 50 kilograms of marijuana.

CONTRIBUTORY NEGLIGENCE

Sadly, dozens of officers die each year in the line of duty, many in high-speed chases. So do innocent bystanders who are struck by these fleeing felons or by those officers in pursuit of them. In many of these cases, defendants attempt to shift the blame to the dead officers and bystanders, suggesting that their actions may have contributed to their own demise.

Case law from North Carolina and all other states left no question that the law of contributory negligence has no place in the criminal laws. Contributory negligence assigns blame in civil cases to the victim of a crash and acts as a complete bar to recovering damages. (Other states have a similar concept called "comparative negligence" that might reduce damages based on a percentage of the fault).

Anthony suggested that Officer Matthews was responsible for his own death by traveling twice the posted speed limit, when he himself was traveling more than three times the limit during the chase. It is easy to second guess the split-second decisions of officers in the calm of an office, your living room, or even in a courtroom. In looking at the reasonableness of their decisions, whether talking about a use-of-force incident or engaging in a chase, prosecutors assess what a similarly situated officer would do if confronted with the same circumstances. We also look to see if they complied with their training and the standards set forth by their internal policies.

Analysis of the response times of six other officers in Wilmington who heard the call and responded to assist reveals that many, if not all, were traveling at high rates of speed, even upwards of 100 mph. Further testimony revealed Matthews was a highly trained officer who kept his car in great working order and was complying with the WPD chase policy during the incident.

Simply put, Officer Matthews was not acting unreasonably, he was acting heroically. We do not second guess the firefighters who ran up the stairs of the Twin Towers any more than we say the officers at WPD were contributorily negligent during the chase. We pay our first responders to take on these risks. When first responders are injured or killed in the performance of those duties, the law will be there to fully protect them and punish those who do them harm. If you flee from the police, you will pay the consequences.

FORESEEABILITY AND PROXIMATE CAUSE

No one suggested that Anthony killed Officer Matthews with express malice or that he targeted anyone for death during the incident. Death was not his aim, but it was a reasonably foreseeable side effect. Under the law, you are responsible not only for the things you intend, but the consequences that can be expected from that conduct.

For example, if a getaway driver joins forces with someone to rob a convenience store and the clerk ends up getting shot and killed, the getaway driver is also guilty of that murder because they not only acted in concert but should have reasonably foreseen that death may result from an armed robbery.

There were plenty of circumstances, both from the night of the incident and in his past, to show that Anthony should be charged under a depraved heart theory. Recall from earlier in the book discussing the Ladder of Guilt that a person can be held responsible for second-degree murder under an implied malice theory when they act in a grossly reckless fashion, or are deliberately bent on mischief, or when they are callously indifferent to the rights and safety of others.

Anthony was deliberately bent on mischief the night he encountered Corporal Richards. Robbing other dealers of more than $30,000 in drugs just moments earlier, he intentionally fled from Richards to avoid appre-hension. During the chase, Anthony drove with wanton disregard for the safety of everyone. He recklessly disregarded the imminent danger that his conduct might cause with the full realization that it would inevitably lead officers to respond at great risk to themselves and others.

Anthony also had a troubled past. He had recently been released from prison after serving ten years for kidnapping and armed robbery in an inci-dent where a co-defendant was killed in Philadelphia after they attempted to flee from police. This meant that he was a free man but would return to prison to serve out his remaining sentence if he violated the law again. His prior bad acts, both on the night of the incident and years earlier in Philadelphia, made it clear that he consciously disregarded the safety of others, and intentionally endangered the lives of officers, to escape the consequences of his criminal conduct. Additionally, no one could better appreciate that running from police might have deadly consequences than a man who spent over a decade in prison for doing it once before.

Proximate cause means "but for" an event having occurred a harm would not have resulted. In lawyer speak, proximate cause is defined as "that which, in a natural and continuous sequence, unbroken by any inde-pendent cause, produces injury and without which the result would not have occurred." Simply put, Officer Matthews would not have been speed-ing to assist a fellow officer (resulting in a crash that caused his death) but for the fact that Anthony sped off and drove recklessly. As such, Anthony proximately caused the death of Officer Matthews.

A defendant who lights a fuse and is far away when a bomb explodes is obviously responsible for the death of victims he never encountered. The fact that Officer Matthews was not right behind Anthony when he crashed was irrelevant and not even surprising. A defendant can outrun an officer but not the officer's radio.

Even if other factors intervene, such as an empty box in the middle of the road, the defendant is not excused from his conduct. Nor does it matter if other factors combined with that initial cause to bring about the death. When Anthony stepped on the gas, the resulting chase was inevitable. Accordingly, he could be held responsible for the foreseeable consequences of his actions even though he never met or even saw the officer he killed.

Anthony was convicted of second-degree murder, felony fleeing to elude causing death, two counts of possession of a firearm by a convicted felon (one for the gun found on the side of the road and another for a gun found in his home during a search after the incident), and possession with intent to distribute marijuana. He was sentenced to nearly 20 years in prison. This precedent-setting case is now followed by courts all over the state to hold people fully responsible for the foreseeable consequences they set in motion, up to and including being charged with murdering someone they never met.

KEY #2: SURROUND YOURSELF WITH THE RIGHT PEOPLE

There are many life lessons that can be taken away from the case studies we just covered. Perhaps the biggest is that because you can be held legally responsible for the actions of others, choosing the right people to surround yourself with is a crucial decision you make in life. The legal principles of "acting in concert" (where you can be held responsible for the decisions your friends make) and the law of "constructive possession" (where you can be held responsible for the illegal contraband your friends may be possessing while you are in their presence) are really just legal terms for what is commonly referred to as "guilt by association."

There is a theory that you will become the average of the five people with whom you spend the most time. Read that sentence again and let it sink in. We often say in court that you are only as good as the company you keep. Who do you spend your time with? If you spend a lot of time with individuals who drink a lot, then you probably will too. If you spend a lot of time with individuals who are lazy, then you too will most likely be lazy. However, if you spend time with individuals who are motivated and try to make good decisions to improve their lives, then most likely you will do the same. The late Pastor Adrian Rogers described this concept in just three words, "Stupid rubs off." When you hang around with people making foolish decisions, you get caught up in the consequences of those foolish decisions or make them yourself.

In the same way surrounding yourself with individuals making bad decisions can affect you negatively, surrounding yourself with individuals making good decisions can positively impact you. Someone once said, "Show me your friends, and I'll show you your future." Look at the caliber of people you are spending time with, and we will know the caliber of person you are.

When it comes to friendships, some are worth keeping and some are not. If you find yourself surrounded by individuals who are not bringing out the best in you, then it's probably best to distance yourself from these individuals. If they're more concerned with partying and living in the moment, then they will become a roadblock between you and good decisions that will help you achieve your purpose and dreams.

In 1951 Solomon Asch conducted an experiment to see how social pressure could influence an individual. To conduct this test, he administered a "line test" to students and had them state which comparison line (A, B, or C) was most like the target line.

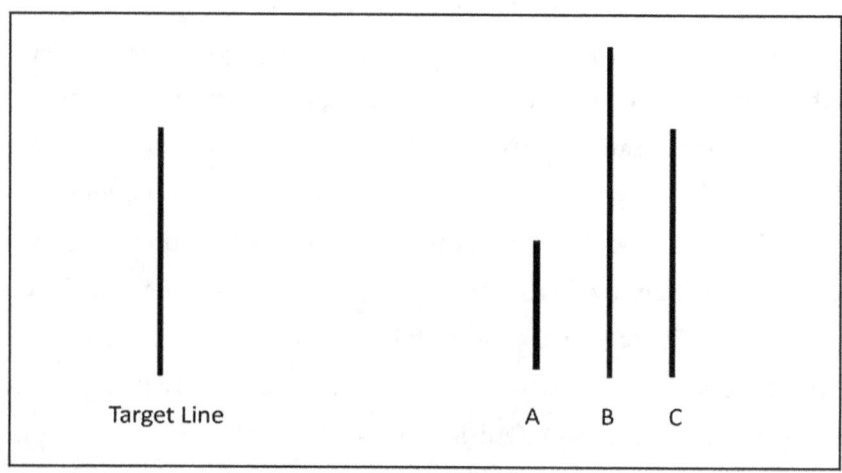

The answer was obvious: C is the correct response. Several of the study participants were instructed to give an incorrect response to see how their answer would influence the decision of the one true participant. The study found that nearly one out of three people were influenced to give an incorrect answer, even though the correct answer was clear, when others around them were consistently picking the wrong responses.[7]

This study illustrates how individuals tend to conform to those around them, even if they know it's wrong. Peer pressure is real because most people have the desire to "fit in." But fitting in with the wrong group of friends is detrimental to a person's future and purpose.

Years ago, Ben went on a safari trip to the Serengeti National Park in Tanzania, Africa. The Serengeti is renowned for its diversity in wildlife and large population of lions. Ben met up with a local guide team and jumped into a reinforced Land Rover and began driving down long dirt roads deep into the savannah where animals were abundant and time seemed to stand still. They were miles away from civilization when one of the tires went flat. They stopped and stepped out to look at the tire and while doing so they looked up and saw a tribe of men approaching them.

Dressed in red, this tribe of men looked rather intimidating as they continued to approach Ben and the guide. One of the natives in Ben's guide group and the leader of these men began having a conversation in their native language as the remaining men began making a circle around Ben and the jeep. This made Ben nervous.

However, what Ben didn't know at the time was that this group of men were of the Maasai tribe. This tribe had hunted lions for centuries. They had hunted lions for so long, in fact, that the lions had developed the ability to smell these men and knew it was best to go the other way when they

---

7   Simply Psychology. (n.d.). Asch conformity experiment. Retrieved from https://www.simplypsychology.org/asch-conformity.html

caught whiff of their odor. You see, at first glance it would appear as if they were forming the circle around Ben and the jeep as a premeditated step to cause him harm, but what they were actually doing was forming a circle around Ben and the jeep to keep the lions from coming out of the high grasses and ambushing them while they were changing the flat tire.

That's what the right friends do. The right friends form a circle around you to keep the "lions" of this world out. We are speaking of the "lions" of bad decisions. Bad decisions with drugs and alcohol. Bad decisions like laziness and cutting corners. Bad decisions like stealing and cheating. Poor choices often arise from self-doubt and a lack of self-confidence. The right friends can help guard against those mistakes, while the wrong friends may open the door for those "lions" to sneak in and cause harm.

One final point about the Maasai. When two men encounter each other, the traditional greeting in their native Swahili is "Kasserian Ingera," which translates to "and how are the children?" The only acceptable response to that question is for the other man, even if he does not have children of his own, to answer "all of the children are well." In the Maasai culture, you are not doing your job as a man if the children in your tribe are hurting. That's knowing your purpose. And those are the kind of men we want to be surrounded by.

SECTION 3

IMPAIRED DRIVING IS NO ACCIDENT

In 2022 there were 13,524 people who died from alcohol impaired driving.[8] That is around 37 deaths a day due to poor decisions. That is a little hard to believe in this day and time when there are so many alternatives to driving while impaired. Each year, roughly one million people are arrested for impaired driving.[9]

[8]   National Highway Traffic Safety Administration. (n.d.). *Drunk driving*. U.S. Department of Transportation. Retrieved [insert retrieval date], from https://www. nhtsa.gov/risky-driving/drunk-driving

[9]   Federal Bureau of Investigation (FBI). Department of Justice (US). Crime in the United States 2016: Uniform Crime Reports. Washington (DC): FBI; 2017. Available at https:// ucr.fbi.gov/crime-in-the-u.s/2016/crime-in-the-u.s.-2016/tables/table-18External. Accessed 16 April 2018.

TIP #4: AVOID IMPAIRED DRIVING

Some of these individuals failed to plan ahead. Some didn't think they were "that drunk." Some thought they could make it home, and some just didn't care. Regardless of the why, this is the deadliest behavior that occurs on our roadways and is easily prevented.

First let's talk briefly about alcohol pharmacology and how it impacts the brain and body. On average, one alcoholic beverage (can of beer, shot of 80 proof whiskey, or glass of wine) raises a person's alcohol concentration to roughly .02. At a .02 a person can generally expect to see changes in judgment and relaxed inhibitions.

Your inhibitions are what keep you from doing things that you know are a bad idea. In other words, a person might be more willing to do something they would ordinarily say is a bad idea. For example, when a person is totally sober, they might say "I will never drink and drive" but after a drink or two that might change to "I don't have to go far" or "I've only had a couple."

If a person continues to drink and their alcohol concentration continues to increase to .05, they will begin to see impairment with their motor skills and poor judgment. If they continue to drink and increase their alcohol concentration to .08, they can expect to see poor coordination, lack of self-control, and poor decision-making.

In the United States most states have a "legal limit" of .08, meaning if your alcohol concentration is .08 or more, you are presumed to be impaired. We put the words "legal limit" in quotations because there are circumstances when a person can be charged and convicted of impaired driving at levels less than .08. The best practice is simply not driving if you're consuming alcohol or any other impairing substances.

Here is what everyone needs to understand about impaired driving: There's no good outcome when someone takes the chance of driving home while drunk or high. There are three possible outcomes. First, you can make it home. That might seem pretty good at first, but the problem is when someone makes it home after driving while impaired, they often reinforce dangerous behavior and think next time they attempt to make it home it will have the same safe outcome. Eventually one of the other two outcomes emerges: Either you get arrested or you become involved in a crash.

The average impaired driving conviction costs around $10,000. That may seem high to some but when you consider court costs, attorney fees, fines, and increased insurance costs over the next few years the grand total comes out to around $10,000 or more. That total would pay for a lot of Uber rides. Not to mention, an arrest never looks good on school and employment applications.

DO NOT CALL IT AN "ACCIDENT"

The worst possible outcome of driving while impaired is becoming involved in a crash, something that really changes lives on all sides, for victims and offenders. We have heard it repeatedly that when this worst-case scenario occurs, people are quick to call it an "accident." Nothing could be further from the truth.

Remember, life is about choices and choices have consequences. People may sincerely regret the consequences - they may even say that they would trade places with the friend they may have just killed and mean it - but they did not make accidents that lead up to these consequences, they made intentional choices.

Try answering these series of questions that an impaired driver might be asked after causing a fatality and see if you agree: Did you accidentally start drinking (or taking drugs) before you got in the car, or was that on purpose? Did you not hear your friends say to call a cab or Uber or that they would drive you back to your home, or did you intentionally disregard that advice? Did you mean to turn on the car, back out of the driveway, shift the car in drive and step on the gas to go down the road, or did the car do that by itself?

You get the point. The answers are obvious. And the consequences of impaired driving are too. In Section II we demonstrated that defendants are held responsible not only for the things that they intended to do (like speeding), but for the foreseeable consequences of their actions (killing an officer). And if someone has already been warned on a prior occasion to "check yourself before you wreck yourself" (possibly through a DWI conviction) and then goes out and offends again it elevates the crime to punishment that few can fathom. The next case illustrates that point.

A JOURNEY FROM AN ACCIDENT TO MURDER

It was a crisp spring Sunday morning, about 10:00 a.m. on April 3, 2011. David and his son, Trey, were riding their bikes down River Road, an 11-mile-long stretch that winds at the start, then parallels the Cape Fear River before meeting Carolina Beach. They were training for a triathlon, a race they had successfully finished in Florida just a year earlier. The scenic views and even terrain made River Road a popular training area for cyclists who traveled this road often. By all accounts, Trey, whose senior prom was a week away and graduation was just after that, could keep up with his dad. They were both the ideal picture of health.

The driver of the vehicle, Thomas, was a study in contrast with David and Trey. A man of 62 years, he had the liver of a much older man, the result of many years of hard drinking. While he had never been charged with driving while impaired (DWI), there were many people who would ultimately come forward to talk about his uncharged exploits. He bragged at bars that he managed his double vision by driving with only one eye open. On a prior occasion, his girlfriend had a panic attack while he swerved to avoid mailboxes while driving on River Road at night. She demanded that he pull over and warned him that he was "going to kill somebody."

Six weeks later, this unfortunate prophecy came true. First on the scene was a truck driver who was on his way home. He called 911. Thomas had been all over the road for miles, swerving into oncoming traffic then veering over the fog line into the grass, traveling long stretches in the dirt before correcting back up on the road. Three women, also cycling on River Road, had to bail into the ditch lining the road to avoid Thomas' car.

Thomas struck David first. David shattered the windshield, rolled over the roof, denting it along the way, and then destroyed the back windshield. He died instantly. Trey, who was in front of his dad, was thrown 187 feet from his bike upon impact. His pulse was weak once help arrived, but he was still alive. Twenty-four hours later his mom watched as he was taken off life support. In a last selfless act, Trey's organs were donated. Thomas tried to flee, but his car was badly damaged, and the trucker's vehicle blocked his path. While others tended to David and Trey, Thomas never left the driver's seat to render aid.

Trooper Bryan Phillips of the State Highway Patrol was one of the first to arrive. The crash reconstruction team that followed Phillips' arrival noted that there were no skid marks on the road or the grass, and no signs of braking to avoid the collision. This was confirmed by Thomas' vehicle's "black box," which showed that the car only slowed upon impact with David and Trey's bodies. Thomas never hit the brakes. Nor did he even slow down before, during, or after hitting David and Trey.

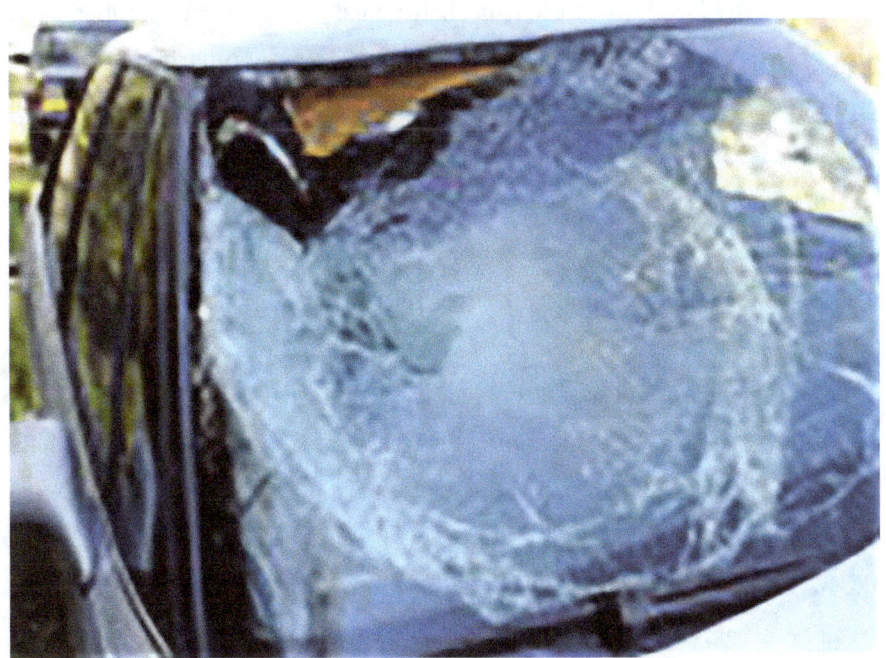

Trooper Phillips was perplexed by his handheld Alco-Sensor reading. Despite smelling of alcohol, Thomas' breathalyzer registered .00. He denied drinking anything since the night before, and while having some indications of impairment, he was able to perform some components of the Standardized Field Sobriety Tests at the roadside. Doubting Thomas' claim that this was all a terrible accident, Trooper Phillips called a certified Drug Recognition Expert to detect if substances other than alcohol might be responsible for his reckless driving. While there were bottles of wine and hard liquor in Thomas' car, the most interesting item for law enforcement was a half-chewed straw with a white substance still in it.

Thomas was transported to the station for further assessment. A sample was drawn for a better reading of his blood alcohol concentration and confirmed the suspicion that other impairing substances were present. His mustache glowed like a Christmas tree when evaluated under a black light. Swabs stuck up his nose indicated the same white substance. Analysts at the North Carolina State Crime Lab revealed that it was mephedrone, also known as "bath salts," which were just gaining popularity at this time and not yet illegal under North Carolina law.

More than 500 investigation hours eventually revealed Thomas' actions in the hours before he ran over David and Trey, elevating the event from a terrible accident to two counts of second-degree murder. The reason we elevated the charges to second-degree murder was the abundant evidence of prior bad acts—Thomas' prior behavior, while not captured in a criminal record, clearly showed a conscious disregard for everyone else and painted the picture of a man who was deliberately bent on mischief. This uncharged 404(b) evidence was the subject of a hearing out of the presence of the jury where we were able to establish many things about Thomas in the hours, days, and even weeks leading up to killing David and Trey.

There were 29 cases in North Carolina that upheld the conviction of the defendant for second-degree murder where the defendant had been convicted of DWI in the past. The theory was that the prior DWI should have put the defendant on notice of the potentially deadly choice of future impaired driving. To consciously disregard it constituted malice.

Thomas had driven impaired on numerous occasions; he openly bragged about being a skilled impaired driver and had been warned by his girlfriend not to drive impaired (on the very road where he would kill David and Trey less than two months later). This was sufficient to supply the malice element for murder, the first of its kind under North Carolina Law.

Additional relevant factors included Thomas' gross level of impairment (analysis of the blood draw showed a blood alcohol concentration of more than twice the legal limit—the breathalyzer Trooper Phillips used at the scene was faulty); the presence of bath salts in his system; his erratic driving earlier that day on River Road that included running three female bikers off the road; his failure to render aid; and his attempt to flee after the fact.

In the weeks that followed, investigators uncovered many other grossly aggravating factors. Thomas' story that he had only two glasses of wine the night before and then went to sleep in his office in Southport (about 30 minutes from Wilmington) was a lie. The schoolteacher with whom he had been on a blind date, and whom he was trying to call at the time of the wreck, confirmed that he drank two glasses of wine at dinner, but his night did not end after that date. A video trained on his bed at the business (which is disturbing) showed that he had not slept there as he claimed. When investigators checked his bank records, an ATM withdrawal of $400 at 4:00 a.m. in northern Wilmington jumped out. Thomas had only $100 in his pocket at the time of the crash. Bars closed at 2:00 a.m. Where did the rest of the money go in the eight hours between the withdrawal and colliding with an innocent father and son on River Road?

It turned out that Thomas had solicited a prostitute named Pat after leaving his date. It was Pat who took Thomas to a drug dealer's house to get the bath salts found in the straw. This was the same substance found in his nose at the time of the incident. Mephedrone is an amphetamine that is "synergistically impairing" with alcohol, according to Dr. William Meggs, East Carolina University Emergency Room Toxicologist who testified at trial. Far from offsetting the depressive effects of alcohol, bath salts amplify the impairment.

Since the time of this case, mephedrone has been declared illegal in North Carolina and in many other states. The world is now aware of the severity of this drug and cases are treated seriously in many jurisdictions.

When it came time for closing arguments, Ben reminded the jury that this was a case about the heart: the broken heart of a mother and wife, the heart of a boy that now beats in the chest of an organ recipient, and the depraved heart of a defendant who took the life of two innocent people. His lack of remorse was heartless.

The jury's verdict was as swift as the judge's sentence was severe. In a case that set precedent, Thomas was convicted of two counts of second-degree murder. Judge Paul Jones ultimately said: "It's sad for everybody that we had to have this trial. I'm a veteran of a lot of trials, over 300 jury trials, and this is one of the saddest. I have presided over 200 murder trials. Some people pled guilty. You pled not guilty, which is your right. Vengeance only belongs to one person, and that's the Lord. But my job is to punish." Judge Jones then sentenced Thomas to consecutive sentences totaling nearly 25 years in prison. Given his age at the time of conviction, he will likely never get out.

DO NOT CALL IT "DRUNK DRIVING"

For years, people have called impaired driving "drunk driving." This is an incorrect term for two important reasons. First, for people who are under the legal age, ANY amount of alcohol is treated as impaired driving–in North Carolina we call it driving after consuming while under 21. That means there is "zero tolerance" for any amount of alcohol in a minor's system and serious criminal consequences and insurance ramifications flow from having even one beer, one shot, any alcoholic beverage even if you are well below .08–which is the "legal limit" in nearly every state.

Second, impaired driving applies to other drugs as well. That is why we called it DWI, "Driving While Impaired," or DUI, "Driving Under the Influence." Over recent years there has been a sharp increase in the number of drug impaired drivers on our roads. This is an especially dangerous trend because whereas people tend to drink alcohol at night, and most commonly take to the streets when bars close at 2:00 a.m., illegal drug use happens throughout the day, when traffic is much higher and innocent children are out and about.

Too many in our society are also over-medicating on muscle relaxers and anxiety medication. Some are hooked on heroin and painkillers. You can find endless statistics to show the numbers that are addicted to these drugs, but those numbers are only the tip of the iceberg due to so many keeping their addiction a secret. Consider this sobering statistic: At the height of the opioid epidemic, more people were dying of overdoses than they were from traffic crashes or gunshots. It is the leading cause of death in America for people under 50. Over 100,000 Americans, that is more than 300 a day, were dying of a drug overdose, mostly from heroin and fentanyl. That's like a plane crashing every day.

It was because of the sharp increase in the numbers of drug impaired drivers that Joe was able to attend Drug Recognition Expert school. DRE school is a program that trains law enforcement officers how to more effectively recognize and collect evidence to successfully prosecute drug impaired drivers. In our world today you're nearly as likely to encounter a drug impaired driver as you are an alcohol impaired driver. According to NHTSA research, in 2020 nearly 60% of drivers seriously injured or killed in traffic crashes tested positive for at least one drug.[10] So you do the math: between alcohol and drug impaired drivers we must be extremely cautious when we get behind the wheel.

---

[10]   United States Department of Transportation, National Highway Traffic Safety Administration, Office of Behavioral Safety Research. (2021). *Update to special reports on traffic safety during the COVID-19 public health emergency: Fourth quarter data [Traffic Safety Facts]* (DOT HS 813 135). https://doi.org/10.21949/1526015

INNOCENCE LOST

Using heroin mixed with fentanyl is suicidal. Driving while on it is homicidal. To save lives, many law enforcement officers carry around Naloxone or Narcan, which can reverse the effects of these drugs and bring people back to life. To encourage people to call 911 when they, or a friend, is experiencing a medical emergency, drug users are given immunity from criminal prosecution in many states for possessing these illegal drugs when first responders receive these medical distress calls.

It's a policy choice made because we want to save people even if they are up to no good. If that means looking the other way on their drug use, we do it. But sometimes these best intentions can also lead to unintended consequences that are too difficult to bear.

On November 1, 2016, Mason was in his car seat. His dad, a long-distance trucker, had the day off and he was running errands with his pregnant wife, and two sons, including Mason who was three days shy of his third birthday. The family car came to a stop at a traffic light near Independence Mall in Wilmington.

Twenty-four-year-old Jonathan grew up in this area of Wilmington and still lived with his parents. His downward spiral through drug addiction, mostly with opioids and heroin, led to various DWI arrests and property offenses. His crimes began to escalate as his breaking and entering charges became a clear sign that his habit had become too expensive to maintain.

Jonathan was not only known to law enforcement as a defendant, he had also been brought back to life with Narcan by police on three different occasions in the previous nine months. Each time he was revived he woke up a free man—the immunity laws meant that officers could not arrest him for the drugs that almost killed him.

Less than two months after Jonathan's most recent overdose, he was once again back on the streets. He now carried a personal Narcan kit in his car in the event he would need to be revived again. On this day, he was again heavily impaired, driving wildly through city streets in a pick-up truck that his family had provided to him.

A Good Samaritan called 911 as Jonathan passed him at an intersection and swerved into the oncoming lane of traffic to pass slower vehicles. The caller reported that the truck he was now intently watching was being driven out of control and it was only a matter of time before there would be real trouble. Less than a minute later, the call proved to be prophetic. Jonathan never stopped at the busy intersection of Independence Boulevard and Oleander Drive, next to the local mall. He slammed full speed into the back of the Richardsons' stopped car. Mason was killed on impact.

As the EMS personnel revived and treated Jonathan for his minor injuries, he asked the first responders if immunity laws would once again protect him from criminal prosecution, confident that this fourth time would be like his three prior events. The answer, of course, was a resounding no—immunity extends to drug possession, not the crimes one might do while impaired. Jonathan was charged with second-degree murder under the same theory of implied malice that had convicted Anthony and Thomas.

A needle found in the vehicle tested positive for fentanyl. Any amount of this substance in the human system is considered DWI – stated another way, there is "zero tolerance" for schedule 1 controlled substances like heroin and fentanyl. Additionally, the trial judge ruled that Jonathan's prior DWI convictions were admissible in evidence to show reckless indifference to consequences. Given all these factors, the jury convicted Jonathan of second-degree murder. He was sentenced to 15-19 years in prison. Mason's family still visits the intersection where the crash occurred to put up balloons every year on his birthday.

Justice officials were devastated by Mason's death and were committed to changing the practice of walking away from overdose revival cases, even if the law still provided immunity for the drug possession offenses that were in plain view. We joined forces with medical professionals and others within the addiction community and created a Quick Response Team (QRT). We believed it was lunacy to allow people like Jonathan to leave without any consequences and with no follow-up support.

Today, when someone is brought back to life with Narcan, the QRT (made up of a peer-support specialist, a licensed therapist, and police officer) arrives at that person's doorstep within 48 hours of the overdose. We also advocate for short term incarceration through the civil laws known as "involuntary commitment" when those we are trying to reach present a clear danger to themselves and others. This new policy has saved countless lives, not only for the people getting treatment, but for those they may harm without that treatment. Stopping drug impaired driving is everyone's business.

THE BILL OF RIGHTS

We have all heard of the Bill of Rights, the First Ten Amendments to the United States Constitution. Many of us know at least a few. The First Amendment grants the right to free speech, freedom of the press, separation of church and state, and freedom of assembly. This is followed by the Second Amendment Right to Bear Arms.

The middle Amendments, the Fourth through the Sixth, come up when an officer stops a citizen on the road. The Fourth Amendment protects citizens from "unreasonable searches and seizures," meaning police officers usually need a search warrant. But there are exceptions such as when time is of the essence and there are "exigent circumstances" and no time to get a warrant (cars by their very nature of being mobile frequently create this situation); "search incident to arrest" where the police can search the contents of the vehicle during an arrest; and when contraband is "in plain view" and there is "no expectation of privacy" because it was left out in the open.

The Fifth Amendment gives a person the "right to remain silent" since citizens are "presumed innocent," while the Sixth Amendment gives citizens the right to be represented by a lawyer. These two amendments are combined in Miranda Warnings: "You have the right to an attorney. You have the right to remain silent. Anything you say can and will be used against you in a court of law..." You have probably heard of these rights before.

Imagine you're driving down the road with friends when the car you are in gets pulled over for a minor traffic violation. You're sitting in the back seat next to a close friend who has been drinking and has illegal drugs in his pocket.

As the officer approaches, he detects the odor of alcohol and asks the driver to step out and perform a Field Sobriety Test (FST), which may include blowing into a breathalyzer to determine if the driver has consumed alcohol. While your friend has a Fifth Amendment right to remain silent and refuse to blow into the machine at the station, driving itself is not a right—it's a privilege. By signing for a driver's license, a driver agrees to certain conditions under what's known as "Implied Consent." One of those conditions is that if an officer requests a breath sample, the driver must comply. Refusing means an automatic one-year license suspension, regardless of the test results.

Now, what about a vehicle search? The officer likely does not need a warrant due to the previously explained legal exceptions, but it does not stop there. While speaking with the driver, the officer glances at the back seat and notices one of the passengers looks extremely nervous. "Is there anything illegal in the car I should know about?" the officer asks. The driver, attempting to stay cool, responds, "No, sir." The officer then follows up: "Would you mind if I search the car?"

Unbeknownst to the group, the nervous passenger is hiding a small amount of illegal drugs in his pocket. The driver, thinking there's nothing to worry about, consents to the search. One by one, the officer asks everyone to exit the vehicle and frisks each person for weapons. As the nervous passenger prepares to step out, what do you think he does with the drugs? Often, someone in this situation will discreetly hide them somewhere in the car before getting out.

Once everyone is out, the officer begins searching the vehicle. As he checks between the front passenger seat and the center console, he finds the drugs that were secretly stashed moments earlier. Holding them up, he asks, "Who do these belong to?"

Do you think anyone speaks up? Most of the time, the answer is no. So, who gets charged? Under the legal principle of "constructive possession" everyone in the car can be arrested. This law holds that if drugs are within your reach and you had the ability to control them, you can be held responsible—even if they were not yours. In an instant, one person's poor decision has affected everyone. In other words, stupid just rubbed off.

At this point, you might be thinking, "That's not fair!" But ask yourself—is life always fair? Just like the legal concept of acting in concert, constructive possession can make you accountable for the people you surround yourself with. That is why it is critical to choose your friends wisely.

And if you're wondering whether you could avoid charges by testifying against the others in the car, that's a possibility—but so is losing your friendships. If you value your future and your friends, keep drugs out of your car and out of your life and do not get in a car when they are around or anyone has been using them.

HAVE AN EXIT STRATEGY

Defensive drivers plan ahead if they plan on consuming alcohol or any other impairing substance. No matter how much they consume they have a plan in place that keeps them from getting behind the wheel if they are consuming any substance that may impact their judgment and reactions. Defensive drivers also know that they must constantly be alert and watchful for other motorists who may be impaired. Not just at night but at all times of the day. They are watchful every time they are behind the wheel.

One final thought on this topic before moving on. Do not get in the car with someone who has been drinking or using other impairing substances. When you get in the car with someone else, you are an observer and simply along for the ride. Have you ever ridden a roller coaster or ride at the fair and wanted the ride to stop before the ride operator decided to stop it? The same is true when you are riding in a car with someone else.

This is why you will find that at the end of this book there is a family driving agreement. We have found that it is a powerful tool to start a conversation about the three keys to decision-making and having a clear path out of danger. If someone you love is in a dangerous situation and needs a ride home, you want the phone to ring, rather than receiving a knock on the door.

KEY #3: EVERY DECISION COMES WITH A CONSEQUENCE

Every decision we make, from seemingly the unimportant decisions to the most important decisions, comes with a consequence. Often when we speak to different groups, we take along a bucket, a golf ball, and a quarter to conduct an exercise that demonstrates how decisions work.

During this exercise we separate the audience into two groups and have them form two parallel lines with one team facing the other team. A bucket is placed at the end of the line and is filled with water and a golf ball is placed inside. We stand at the other end of the line between the two teams.

Once both teams have closed their eyes, we flip a coin and show the coin to the two team members standing at the very back of the line. If the coin lands with heads up their goal is to squeeze the shoulder of the person standing next to them. Once that person feels the squeeze, they will squeeze the shoulder of the person standing next to them. The squeezes continue down the line until eventually the persons standing next to the bucket feel the squeeze and at that point their job is to retrieve the golf ball from the bucket of water before the other team. The team that retrieves the golf ball gets a point. The first team to earn three points is the winning team.

But there are a couple of rules to this game. Number one, you can't talk. If anyone on either team speaks during the exercise, the other team automatically gets the point. Number two, participants should only squeeze the shoulder of the person next to them if the coin lands heads up. If someone squeezes on tails, the squeezes will continue down the line until eventually the person at the end of the line retrieves the golf ball from the water bucket. In this case, the opposing team would be awarded the point because they are only supposed to squeeze on heads. Inevitably, someone always gets in a hurry and inadvertently squeezes on tails to be first. Once the first squeeze has occurred, there's no stopping the squeezes until someone grabs the golf ball.

This exercise is a great illustration of how decisions work. When someone makes a decision, it sets in motion a chain of events that ultimately ends with a consequence. When the consequence is bad, that person cannot go back and change it. That's why it's so important to make the right decision to start with. Also, this exercise illustrates that one person's poor decision to squeeze on tails has an impact on the rest of the team. When one person makes a bad decision, it can impact many others.

SECTION 4

MORE DRIVING TIPS TO KEEP YOU SAFE

So far, we have covered the fatal three--distracted driving, speeding, and impaired driving. You have now encountered many bad stories that tell you what NOT to do. We also covered the three keys to decision-making that will hopefully keep the lions away: know your purpose, surround yourself with the right people, and remember that choices have consequences. In this final section, we are going to cover what you SHOULD do behind the wheel. These are more driving tips designed to keep you safe.

TIP #5: WEAR YOUR SEATBELT

This tip may seem obvious, and hopefully it is, but in our careers, we have heard every excuse in the book when on the roadside or in a courtroom for why people did not buckle up. "It wrinkles my blouse," "It scratches my neck," "I have a medical condition," and "I forgot" were some of the most common excuses. And then there is the granddaddy of them all: "You're just as likely to be injured because you're wearing your seatbelt." Someone who says this will then go into a story about their brother's friend's cousin's sister who was in a crash and would've been killed if they had been wearing their seatbelt.

It's just not true. We have handled thousands of cases and gone to many fatalities in our combined half century of seeing the worst traffic crashes. In almost every case, whether it was a fatality or serious injury we would say "they would've been much better off wearing their seatbelt." Current research indicates that you reduce the risk of moderate injury or death by 45%-65% by putting on your seatbelt.[11]

Two other points. First, the shoulder strap is meant to go across the center of your chest (sternum) and not under your arm or behind your

---

[11] National Highway Traffic Safety Administration. (n.d.). *Seat belts*. U.S. Department of Transportation. Retrieved February 23, 2025, from https://www.nhtsa.gov/vehicle-safety/seat-belts

head. Wearing a seatbelt incorrectly increases the likelihood of breaking your ribs and puncturing your lungs. Second, seatbelts are designed to work as a system in conjunction with airbags. Airbags alone aren't enough. Wearing your seatbelt is a habit that's easily formed by putting it on every time you get into a car.

Finally, do not forget about your passengers. Make it a habit to ask your passengers to buckle up because you oversee the vehicle you operate. For those of you who are new parents, make sure that the rear-facing baby seat that holds your whole world is installed correctly. Believe it or not, a recent study found that a large percentage of them are misinstalled, meaning they may not work correctly in a crash.[12] Visit www.nhtsa.gov to find a car seat inspection station in your area.

---

[12]   National Highway Traffic Safety Administration. (2022). *Car seat safety: Correct car seat use*. U.S. Department of Transportation. Retrieved from https://www.nhtsa.gov

TIP #6: AVOID UNPROTECTED LEFT TURNS ACROSS BUSY STREETS

Left turns can be extremely dangerous. Mainly because if your vehicle is struck in the passenger side or driver's side door by a vehicle traveling more than 35 mph there's a good chance someone is going to be injured or killed. These crashes often occur when drivers fail to see oncoming traffic, or they misjudge a gap in traffic.

Avoid making unprotected left turns across busy, multi-lane roads. Unprotected left turns occur when someone is turning left without the presence of a traffic signal with a green arrow. They can also occur when turning left at an intersection when you have a green light or a flashing yellow arrow or when you're turning left out of a driveway or business parking lot. It may be better to take a few extra moments to turn right and find a safer area to turn around or take a slightly different route than to risk becoming involved in a crash.

When we do have to make unprotected left turns it's important that we don't let the driver behind us pressure us into making our turn when we're not comfortable. You might look in the rear-view mirror and see the driver behind you throwing their hands up in frustration because they're in a hurry and they want you to turn. Or that same driver may honk the horn at you to get you to go. Don't let them pressure you into going if you're not comfortable making the turn. If a crash does occur, they will not stick around and take any responsibility. You will take all responsibility for the crash.

Along the same lines, if you can't see what's coming, don't go. A lot of times while we are preparing to make left turns other vehicles can obstruct our view. Take the picture below. The person driving the van in this picture can't see oncoming traffic due to stopped traffic, but they decided to pull out anyway. Fortunately, the cars didn't collide, but oncoming traffic had to stop quickly to avoid hitting the van.

So, what are our lessons here?

1) When in doubt, wait. If you're not sure you have enough of a gap between traffic to make your turn, just WAIT.

2) If you cannot clearly see oncoming traffic, just WAIT.

3) It may make take a few extra minutes, but right turns are safer than left turns

4) Defensive drivers should be very cautious when approaching gaps in traffic where other cars may pull out and into their path. When approaching these gaps, slow down and cover the brake, which means having your foot over the brake and being prepared to apply it if necessary.

A final thought relating to turning: Never trust another vehicle's turn signal. Often, many drivers waiting to make a turn onto another street will see a vehicle approaching with their turn signal on and automatically think that it's safe for them to complete their turn. Remember, sometimes drivers mistakenly activate their turn signals, put them on too early, or aren't even aware that their signal is on and have no intention of turning. Before turning out make sure the approaching vehicle is committed to turning.

Bonus Tip: When preparing to turn, keep your wheels straight until you begin the turn. If you're stopped and waiting to make a left turn, turning your wheels in advance can be dangerous. If you're rear-ended while your wheels are turned, your vehicle could be pushed into oncoming traffic. Keeping your wheels straight helps reduce that risk.

TIP #7: HANDLING TAILGATERS

It doesn't take long after you begin driving to find out how many impatient and inconsiderate people are out there. You can't avoid tailgaters, so how do you handle them?

First, do not "brake check" a tailgater by tapping your brakes intentionally to get them to slow down and back off. We can be held responsible when our brake check causes another car to crash into us. In fact, some states have safe movement violations that ultimately indicate that if a driver stops or slams on brakes without reason, they can be held at least partially responsible–not only civilly, but criminally when serious injury or death occurs. If you search the internet for "brake check leads to crash" you will get several attorney websites willing to help you file a civil suit if you were in a crash because of someone "brake checking" you.

So, what should we do? First, start by increasing your following distance between your vehicle and the vehicle ahead of you. If your original following distance was three seconds between your car and the vehicle ahead, you should increase that distance to at least four seconds. We do this because an increased following distance allows us to make more gradual and slower stops. By making more gradual and slower stops we give the tailgating driver behind us more time to recognize that we are stopping and take the appropriate action which hopefully means they avoid crashing into us.

Second, we should hug the right edge of our lane or roadway. This is done for two reasons. First, it puts us closer to a possible escape route if we must drive off the roadway or steer right out of our lane to avoid being rear ended. Second, it allows the driver behind us to see the brake lights of the vehicle ahead of us so they can more quickly notice that traffic ahead is stopping and take the appropriate action.

Next, if a vehicle is following so closely that you find yourself heavily distracted by that vehicle or simply feel uncomfortable and unsafe, pull off the roadway into a nearby parking lot and let them pass. We get it, it's infuriating when someone is obnoxiously tailgating you, especially if it causes you to be inconvenienced because they're being a jerk. But stay focused on the big picture. Our job is to arrive at our destination safely. Don't lose sight of that goal. That's why we always leave a few minutes early. Defensive drivers keep the big picture in mind and plan accordingly.

TIP #8: AVOIDING HEAD-ON COLLISIONS

Head-on collisions account for only a small percentage of all crashes on our roadways but when they do occur, they often result in serious injury or death. Typically, head-on collisions result from one of three causes: 1) A confused driver (elderly or other cognitive disability), 2) A drug or alcohol impaired driver, or 3) A distracted driver. A confused or impaired driver may mistakenly enter a highway and travel in the wrong direction. On two-lane roads, distracted drivers who take their eyes off the road often veer into oncoming traffic.

In 2007, a young college student named Annie made the responsible choice to be the designated driver for her friends who had been drinking. After ensuring that her friends got home safely, she got into the backseat of another friend's car for a ride to her own apartment. Around 2:00 a.m., as they drove home, a young man who had been drinking heavily and was traveling over the speed limit lost control of his vehicle. Whether he passed out or simply failed to maintain control, we couldn't be sure. As he sped downhill, he crossed the median into oncoming traffic and collided head-on with the car Annie was traveling in. The violent impact propelled her forward, causing her head to strike the back of the driver's seat, breaking her neck and ultimately taking her life. The young man was charged and convicted of Felony Death by Motor Vehicle and sentenced to prison.

So, what can you do to help avoid head-on collisions? Here are some tips that might help:

1) Drive in the right lane. On multi-lane roads, use the far-right lane whenever possible. When drivers become confused, whether they are impaired cognitively or by a substance, and they begin traveling in the wrong direction they often choose the left lane (left lane when you're traveling the correct direction). By driving in the right lane, it will hopefully help you avoid these drivers.

2) Reduce your speed. If you notice a vehicle traveling in your lane head-on, the first action you should take is to reduce your speed in a controlled manner. Less speed will afford you more time to react and reduce the force of impact if you crash. Control your deceleration so you can control your vehicle. Don't come to a complete stop. If you come to a complete stop, you lose your mobility.

3) Try to get the other driver's attention. Flash your headlights or even honk your horn. Hopefully this will get the attention of the other driver and they will return to their lane without incident.

4) Steer away. If you take the above actions with no response from the other vehicle you are forced to steer away. Usually, the best option is steering to the right. There are always exceptions to this rule, but most often the best option is to go to the right. If you go to the left, you run the risk of causing another head-on collision with other vehicles even if you miss the vehicle traveling in your lane. Also, when the person driving in your lane realizes they are on the wrong side of the road they will most likely steer or swerve back to their right.

Steer right but do so in a controlled, smooth manner. It's usually better to strike a mailbox or end up in a ditch opposed to striking another vehicle head-on. Try to avoid fixed objects such as trees or concrete culverts that will bring you to an immediate stop and can cause significant injury or death.

5) Do not over-correct. If you drive off the road and are attempting to bring your vehicle back onto the road, remember to not jerk the wheel back to the left. Instead, take your foot from the accelerator, and allow the vehicle to slow naturally if possible. If you must brake, try to do so gradually. If it's safe to re-enter the road, steer back to the left smoothly and don't jerk the wheel. In some cases, it may be best to come to a stop along the side of the road and collect yourself.

6) Make it a glancing blow. If a collision is imminent, try to make it a glancing blow. Usually when you're involved in a collision of any kind the more gradual you can stop after impact the better off you are. In other words, would you rather go from 50 mph to 0 mph instantly or 50 mph to 0 mph over the course of a few seconds?

The earlier you can identify a vehicle traveling at you head-on the better off you are. Defensive drivers should stay alert and identify potential hazards as early as possible. Be aware when driving late at night that you may be more likely to encounter impaired drivers.

TIP #9: ALWAYS KNOW YOUR LOCATION

This tip is a lesson Joe learned as a police officer. One of the first things law enforcement officers are taught is to always know your location in case an emergency arises. The last thing you want is to be in a fight for your life and not be able to tell your back-up your location. The same principle applies when you're driving. If you are involved in a crash or you must call 911 in an emergency, you need to know your location immediately.

You might say "I will just pull up my location on my phone." Here's the problem with that strategy: in a crash, phones often go flying. Once you find your phone you still must open the apps on your phone and then zoom in to identify your location. This can take several seconds if not a minute or more. In an emergency seconds feel like minutes and minutes feel like hours. You need to have your location information immediately available.

Here are a few tips to always ensure you know your location:

1) Pay attention to street signs. Obviously, street signs give you your location, but many people overlook other important information on many street signs like block numbers.

Take the picture above for example. If we were to turn right onto Wilshire Blvd, we would be in the 4500 block of Wilshire Blvd. If we were to turn left, we would either be in the 4400 block of Wilshire Blvd or the 4600 block depending on the street. These block numbers progress sequentially as you pass other side streets. In an emergency if you called 911 you could tell them you witnessed a crash in the 4600 block of Wilshire Blvd, and they would know exactly where to send help.

2) Pay attention to the businesses. When you call 911, they can often determine your location if you give them the name of the nearest business. You will also want to pay attention to the addresses posted on the front of businesses. Businesses often do a good job of posting their addresses because they want their potential customers to be able to find them.

3) Pay attention to exit numbers and mile markers. When traveling on the highway make sure to pay attention to the exit numbers and mile markers because sometimes all you can see when traveling down the highway is asphalt and trees. Most drivers are pretty good at paying attention to the exit numbers but many overlook mile markers.

Take this picture for example. If this mile marker was not present it would be difficult to give your location in an emergency. In the event you need to call for help when traveling down the highway you also need to be able to tell them the direction you're travelling in (north, south, east, or west).

Many drivers tend to focus their attention on other things when they're driving. They think about their work, their music, or their friends and family and often overlook the importance of always knowing their location. When an emergency does arise, and it will, you need to be able to give your location as quickly as possible.

TIP #10: MAINTAIN YOUR VEHICLE

Driving a vehicle that needs maintenance, and repair is a lot like shooting a gun with an obstructed barrel. It's unsafe. Would you ride a roller coaster that twists and turns along a narrow track if it needed repair? Of course not. The same should apply to our vehicles as well. When we drive a vehicle that has not been taken care of and maintained, we are increasing the likelihood that we will become involved in a crash. Some parts and systems of our cars are more important than others. If the radio isn't working that may take some of the joy from driving, but at least it doesn't impact the way the vehicle handles and responds. Here are some of the most important parts of our vehicle that we need to maintain to keep us and everyone else safe on the roads.

1) Tires. The tires on your vehicle are perhaps the most important aspect of your vehicle's control system. We should check that our tires have proper air pressure and tread depth at least once each month.

Correct air pressure helps to ensure that the vehicle handles correctly and increases the life of our tires. If we have too much air pressure, we will wear out the middle of the tire before wearing out the outer edges. If we have too little air pressure, we will wear out the edges of the tire before we wear out the middle of the tire. Correct air pressure causes the tires to be worn evenly and last longer. Tires that are worn excessively are more likely to result in "blow-outs," sudden escape of the air from our tire as it ruptures.

Blow-outs can be extremely dangerous especially at higher speeds. The faster you are traveling the less control you have. That is why you should always inspect your tires several days before taking a long trip. This will allow you time to get worn tires replaced. If you are driving and suffer a blow-out expect your car to pull to one side or even want to rotate. The last thing you should do if this occurs is jam on the brakes. If a tire blows out, take your foot off the accelerator and let the car begin to slow naturally. If you must apply the brakes, do so very gradually. As your vehicle is slowing, steer to the right if it's clear and gradually bring the car to a stop along the side of the road.

Also, make sure your vehicle is equipped with a spare tire, lug wrench, and jack, and that your spare tire is fully inflated. Tow truck operators often tell us that many drivers don't realize they lack a spare tire—or that it's flat—until they're stranded on the side of the road.

Another important aspect of your tires is making sure they have proper tread depth. Many drivers don't even realize the purpose of tread and believe its main purpose is to grip the roadway. But think about this: NASCAR drivers speed around a track at nearly 200 mph on slick tires without any tread. The flatter the tire the more contact it has with the roadway surface which generates more friction. More friction helps to ensure your vehicle stays on the roadway. So why do you need tread on your tires? The tread displaces water when driving on wet roads. When you drive through a puddle the water can flow through the tread and the tire can still stay in contact with the roadway surface. If you have bald or slick tires, your tires may skip across the top of the water causing you to hydroplane and lose control of the vehicle.

To make sure your tires have sufficient tread start by finding the wear bars or wear indicators. They are found between the tread at different spots around the tire. Often, small arrows or initials on the side of the tire indicate the location of these indicators.

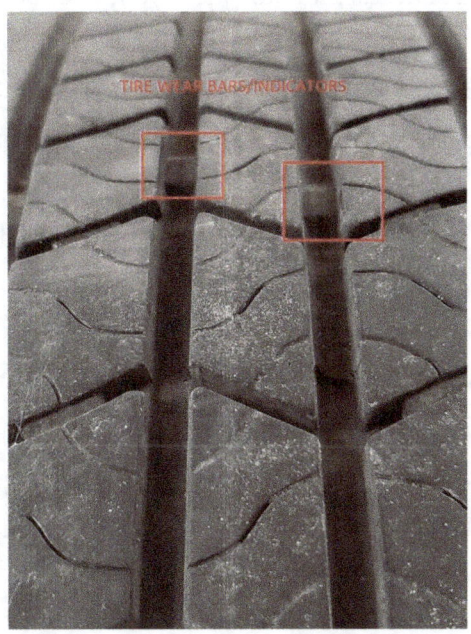

Notice the red squares highlighting the wear bars above. When the tread wears down and becomes even with the wear bars it's time to replace your tire.

Your tires are crucial to your safety. Make sure they have sufficient air pressure and tread depth to increase the odds you arrive at your destination safely.

2)   Brakes. If we must explain the importance of having safe, properly functioning brakes then we have a lot of work to do to make you a defensive driver. Worn out brakes can make the difference between crashing into a car or person and avoiding trouble. How do you know when it's time to replace your brake pads? It's not very hard. Usually, they let you know when it's time by making an annoying squealing sound every time you stop. This sound is caused by a metal shim or indicator in the brake pad that contacts the rotor when your pads become worn down. When you hear this screeching noise it's time to replace your brake pads. When you hear the screeching noise, take your car to a mechanic. If you hear a grinding noise, definitely take your car to a mechanic.

Also, it's a good idea to have your brake fluid checked each time you take your car in for an oil change. Lack of brake fluid can lead to brake failure.

3)   Wipers. If you're going to drive safely you must be able to see. If your wipers are beginning to dry rot or crack it is time to replace them. If they're not sufficiently clearing your windshield when needed, it is time to replace them. Wipers are some of your vehicle's least expensive parts, but they have a very important role. Do not wait for a rainy day before replacing them. When you notice that it's time to replace them go ahead and spend the $40 and get new ones.

4)   Headlights. Clear functioning headlights are essential at night. A study by AAA found that headlights that have become hazy and yellowed over time may only emit 20% of the light they once

did when they were new.[13] The earlier we can identify a potential threat or hazard the more likely we are to safely avoid that hazard. Clear, well working headlights allow you to see further ahead and thereby identify hazards more quickly and easily. If your headlights are becoming cloudy and less effective you can try buying a restoration kit to clear the exterior of your headlights or you may need to buy a new headlight assembly. These can be a little pricey but well worth the expense considering what they do.

It is impossible to be a defensive driver if you're driving an unsafe vehicle. There's a saying: "Take care of your equipment and your equipment will take care of you." This is true for your vehicle. If you want to stop quickly, you need good brakes. If you want your car to handle properly, make sure your tires and suspension system are in good working order. If you want the best possible visibility, make sure your headlights and windshield wipers are in good working order and are functioning as they should be.

---

[13]   Consumer Reports. Old Headlights Can Be Dangerously Dim, Study find. Located at: https://www.consumerreports.org/car-repair-maintenance/old-headlights-can-be-dangerously-dim/. Accessed on: 4/13/20.

TIP #11: PLAN YOUR ROUTE IN ADVANCE

This tip is primarily for new drivers or anyone who is driving in an unfamiliar city or town. It can be extremely stressful when you are traveling in heavy traffic and you're not sure which lane you need to be in. Next thing you know you need to make a lane change but are prevented from doing so by other cars. As a result, you find yourself making a risky lane change to stay on the path you need to be on.

To avoid the stress that comes along with driving on unfamiliar streets plan in advance. Before leaving, pull up your map app on your phone and plan your route. Learn where you need to turn and look for landmarks that will show when and where those turns are approaching. Zoom in using your map app and learn what lane you need to be in to make your turn. Also look to see what lanes end or change into turn lanes so you don't find yourself surprised. Usually there are signs that indicate a lane is ending so make sure to pay attention for those. Plan your route ahead of time to minimize reliance on your GPS and never program it while driving.

If you find yourself in the wrong lane at an intersection–for example you need to be in the turn lane but you are currently in the straight lane– do not inconvenience others by putting on your signal and waiting for an opening to change lanes while your light is green and the traffic behind you is waiting to go straight ahead. Instead, just go straight and find a street or driveway that you can use to turn around and get back on track.

TIP #12: AVOID ROAD RAGE SITUATIONS

In today's world there are so many people struggling with emotional and psychological disorders as well as anger issues and general impatience. As a defensive driver you must avoid confrontations on the road and avoid instigating confrontations. If someone cuts you off in traffic, let it go. If someone is tailgating you, follow Tip #7 but don't brake check them and run the risk of causing a confrontation. Stay focused on the big picture.

The big picture is making it to your destination safely. You never know who has weapons in their car or who's just having a bad day and may over-react to a situation. Let it go! Let them pass, pull off the road for a moment, don't let your ego get the best of you. In a popular commencement speech, Dr. Rick Rigsby said, "Ego is the anesthesia that deadens the pain of stupidity." Getting into a confrontation on the road is just simply a stupid thing to do. Unfortunately, road rage incidents are all too common.

In the summer of 2021, the streets of Wilmington became the backdrop for a tragic encounter between two strangers, forever altering the course of their lives and taking the life of an innocent person. Thomas, aged 25, found himself in a heated confrontation with William, a 43-year-old prison guard, after an abrupt lane change left one man feeling disrespected. What began as a moment of road rage escalated into a reckless display of speed, with both men pushing their vehicles to nearly 80 mph in a misguided contest of dominance.

In the chaos of their reckless driving, Thomas collided with a car driven by a 79-year-old man who was killed on impact. Both men were charged with involuntary manslaughter and a slew of traffic offenses under a theory of acting in concert that we discussed in Section 2. William pled guilty to reckless driving and lost his job even though his car was not directly involved in the collision. Thomas was convicted of involuntary manslaughter and sentenced to prison. Neither man had ever met each other or the man they killed and yet in a fleeting moment of anger, they set the wheels in motion to an event that spiraled out of control.

So, what should you do if you inadvertently find yourself in a road rage situation? Let it go. Do not risk getting in legal trouble or injured over something that's foolish to start with. Call 911 and get help on the way. Avoid these situations. They are dangerous and can be deadly.

TIP #13: PROTECT YOURSELF FINANCIALLY

When drivers make poor decisions, they can be very costly. Not only in terms of lives and injuries but financially as well. Different states have different requirements for insurance, but the main goal is to protect you and your family financially. To illustrate this point, let's look at two actual crashes that we encountered that put families in a terrible position financially.

In the first case, a young woman named Maria was driving when her vehicle was struck by an impaired driver. She suffered devastating injuries in the crash but survived and incurred over $600,000 of medical expenses. The other driver did not have any insurance on the vehicle even though it was required by North Carolina law. (Even though many states require all vehicles to be insured, you would be astounded how many individuals let their insurance lapse and are not carrying any.) The impaired driver also didn't own anything or have any money. He wasn't going to make any money because he was heading off to prison for the next several years. In essence he was liable but was judgment proof. Fortunately, Maria had insurance in the event that she was involved in a collision with an "uninsured or underinsured" person. If she had not had this insurance, her family would have faced financial disaster.

The second case involved two 18-year-old friends who were out late one night riding around after they both had been drinking. The driver began to drive at a high rate of speed and ultimately lost control and crashed into a tree. Tragically the passenger died in the crash.

The driver was sentenced to prison. But it did not end there. His parents were sued in civil court. They faced liability because they hosted the party where the young men were provided with alcohol. This is a theory known as "dram shop" or "social host" liability. As a result, this young man's parents have lost nearly everything they have spent their lives working for. We don't like to think that our children would make these terrible decisions, but unfortunately it happens, and we should plan for the worst-case scenario.

Being a defensive driver means you take measures to protect yourself and your family. Not just when you are behind the wheel but even when you are evaluating your insurance coverage and considering foreseeable consequences. If you have not had an evaluation of your policy lately, it's probably a good time to do it. If the unthinkable does happen you will be glad you did.

TIP #14: DON'T DRIVE IN ANOTHER DRIVER'S BLIND SPOT

Even though drivers are taught to always check their blind spots before changing lanes, you can never trust that people are going to do what they are supposed to do. Many of us have experienced driving down a multi-lane highway and having the vehicle next to us begin to change into our lane without even recognizing that we are beside them. Turn signals and blind spots fall into the same category. They are both easy tasks to complete but drivers routinely bypass these safety precautions.

Defensive drivers prepare for others cutting corners but don't cut corners themselves. Make sure to use your signals and check your blind spots when making lane changes. If you notice that you are in another vehicle's blind spot you should either speed up or slow down to avoid this potentially dangerous area. If they come over into your lane you may need to honk your horn, reduce your speed quickly, or even steer away if possible.

TIP #15: EXPECT OTHER DRIVERS TO MAKE MISTAKES

This final tip is the catchall and sums up the concept of defensive driving: we must drive expecting other drivers to make mistakes or to make bad decisions. Stated another way, you can be 100% in the right and still 100% dead or seriously injured through no fault of your own.

We should assume that every time we drive, we will encounter a driver who is distracted and going to run through a red light. We should assume that we will encounter a driver who is in a hurry and tailgating us driving down the road. We should assume that we will encounter an impaired driver crossing into our lane and approaching us head-on. By assuming these situations, we should apply all our experience and knowledge that we have learned and take precautions. Put on our seatbelt, drive at a safe speed, always leave ourselves an escape route, avoid distractions, and think ahead–constantly asking ourselves "what will I do if this happens?"

If driving is a large part of how you make your living, you should consider finding ways to keep your skills sharp. If you are a traveling salesperson or spend hours on the road each day you may be more at risk than other drivers. Not only because you have more exposure but often because you are more tempted to multitask when driving to save time. As we mentioned earlier, this can be a recipe for disaster. Sometimes we need reminders of how dangerous our roads can be even if we have been driving for many years. You might even consider taking an in-person defensive driving class if there's one available near you. Our online defensive driving classes are always available at nationalcpp.org. Continuing education is a great way to fight complacency behind the wheel. Stay safe by staying sharp.

PUT TRAUMA IN THE TRUNK

The reckless behavior that we have been talking about in these pages may be a one-time event, but frequently it is a pattern of behavior that is all too foreseeable. The revolving door at the courthouse that we have witnessed throughout our careers brings in lots of new faces, but we also see many of the same people repeatedly. Do you or someone you love always find trouble? Many people who engage in a consistent pattern of reckless behavior do so because they have yet to confront the toxic stress that may have been a large part of their childhood. Our final piece of advice is to know yourself and put trauma in the trunk.

The case studies in this book involve single traumatic events–life altering, and life taking incidents–that occur in a single second. Medical professionals call this "acute trauma." But there is a second type of trauma, one that is more hidden, less talked about, and leads to far greater destruction. It is called "toxic stress." Instead of a broken arm or bloody lip, there are some people who live with trauma every day.

For kids who grow up in an abusive household or a high poverty neighborhood where violence is ever present, trauma is not confined to an event but is a part of life. In other words, it is not just "one bad hour" but rather "one bad childhood." Over time this toxic stress quite literally changes their body chemistry and their brain functioning.

These children are in a survival mode response to this stress that not only affects them physically (increasing their heart rate, blood pressure, breathing and muscle tension) but mentally (reducing the ability to respond, learn, and maintain relationships and increasing the likelihood of fighting or acting out). These are the "social determinants of health" which turn out to be highly related to the "root causes of crime."

In the mid-1990s, two doctors, Dr. Robert Adna and Dr. Vincent Felitti, began taking a different kind of patient history that did not focus on traditional things like the prevalence of heart disease and cancer in a family. Instead, they conducted a study of thousands of participants to investigate childhood abuse and neglect and their tie to later in life health conditions. Through this work, they developed an assessment tool to measure Adverse Childhood Experiences and Adverse Community Environments (ACEs). They used this data to come up with an ACE score that can draw connections between adverse childhood experiences and medical, social, and economic adversity later in life.

The assessment tool asked 10 yes/no questions and generated an ACE score based on questions answered in the affirmative. Study participants were asked:

1. Are your parents divorced?
2. Is either parent incarcerated?
3. Have you witnessed domestic violence in your home?
4. Is there drug use in your home?
5. Do you suffer from food insecurity or lack of basic needs?
6. Do you lack emotional support from family at home?
7. Is there someone with mental illness in your home?
8. Have you been threatened or emotionally abused at home?
9. Have you been physically abused?
10. Have you been sexually abused?

A child who answers four or more of the 10 questions with a "yes" has a challenging future to confront. They are 70% more likely to be victims or defendants of a violent crime. They are much more likely to become pregnant as teenagers, drop out of high school, or commit suicide. 62% of intravenous drug users have an ACE score of five or higher. Living with this toxic stress has long-term implications on health that leaves a dark legacy with a much greater rate of diabetes and heart disease, to name just a few. The life expectancy of someone who answers yes to six or more questions has a life expectancy of 20 years less than a person who answers zero or one of the questions in the affirmative.

What does that look like over time? In our combined experience we have seen young people living with toxic stress who become the adults living on a cul-de-sac of despair. They are in a vicious loop that puts them in the never-ending cycle of bad relationships and bad choices, where today's victim becomes tomorrow's defendant. You have read about some of them in this book. And when people are in pain, they tend to look for medication. Many, we have come to learn, find heroin. Many choose destructive relationships.

Does this hit close to home? The people we encountered in a lot of impaired driving cases, and reckless behavior behind the wheel, were more susceptible to poor decision-making because they were likely dealing with unresolved and untreated trauma.

Now here is the great news. A child is not washed up at age seven or beyond repair at age 12. The clay that is their brain is still being shaped. Children are resilient, and we can change the arc of their future if we change their present circumstances.

This lesson is powerfully demonstrated in "Resilience: The Biology of Stress and the Science of Hope," a documentary by Drs. Anda and Felitti that discusses their groundbreaking work that can lead to far better outcomes. With the right support structure in place those with high ACE scores can not only succeed but can flourish because "adversity builds character." If you are an older person with a high ACE score who has succeeded, it is almost certainly because you had a support system in place that offset the trauma that was all around you.

A high ACEs score is not a death sentence, it is a diagnosis that can lead to early intervention and effective treatment. Many of the heroic first responders and criminal justice professionals we have worked alongside for years have high ACE scores. For them, early adversity was overcome by even better support. There is a scale to measure resilience, which includes having a resilient caregiver, building social connections, meeting basic needs, and building social and emotional skills. By pairing ACE scores with resiliency scores, one can assess the tools that an individual needs to respond to their ACEs. In other words, a high resiliency score can help to combat a high ACE score.[14]

Positive childhood experiences (PACEs) can overcome ACEs. There are individual protective factors and community protective factors that can build up resilience in individuals, even those who have experienced great trauma as children. The key for children is having at least one caring adult in their lives. Maybe that is you. And if you need help, know that you are not alone in facing your challenges.

What ultimately overcomes this trauma is a belief that your future can be better than your present circumstances and that you have a role in shaping that future. That is called hope. When an individual becomes hope centered, they think about the future and start to make decisions that make that future brighter. It is possible to go from being a survivor to becoming a thriver.

Trauma looks out the rear-view mirror. It is what has happened to you. But hope looks out the windshield. It is what is possible. As you journey

---

[14]   "Got Your ACE Score?" *Aces Too High*, https://acestoohigh.com/got-your-ace-score/.

down the road of life, that trauma, caused by the toxic stress, will always remain in the car with you. But when you become hope centered, you can move that trauma from the driver's seat and put it in the trunk.[15] A good start to taking control of the wheel is by focusing on the tips and life lessons we have laid out in this book.

We are proud to live in the only state in the country that currently has an ACEs informed court system. We have tried to put many of these best practices into our work when we talk about driver safety and decision-making. We are passionate about protecting lives by empowering people to make better choices.

This book and video series have enabled us, through the non-profit The National Crash Prevention Program (NCPP), to continue the goal of educating the public, especially those dealing with high stress like our children, first responders, and members of the military. We hope that you now also have better tools to become a more defensive driver and make better decisions in general. Thank you for taking this journey with us. Travel happy and safe down the road of life.

---

[15] Gwinn, Casey. *Hope Rising: How the Science of Hope Can Change Your Life*. Penguin Random House, 2020.

This Family Driving Agreement is something we highly encourage families with young drivers to complete together. We believe that parents make the best police and that young people hunger for an adult conversation. If you are not talking to your kids, someone else will. Once completed, post it on your refrigerator as a daily reminder of the expectations and responsibilities that come with driving. To get a clean version of the agreement and to see our most up to date forms, please visit our website at www.nationalcpp.org.

FAMILY DRIVING AGREEMENT

This agreement is intended for families with new, inexperienced drivers. Its overall intent is to produce safer drivers by setting expectations and rules that are agreed upon as a family. Feel free to amend this document to best fit the needs of your family. Make sure to discuss the rules and expectations as a family to ensure the agreement is fully understood by all. Fill it out in ink and keep it in a place that is highly visible so it will serve as a reminder to the entire family.

New Driver's Name: _____

1)   As a driver, I recognize the importance and my responsibility to follow the rules and laws of the road. _____ (Initials)

2)   As a driver, I recognize that making poor decisions can have significant impacts on my life and my family's life. _____ (Initials)

3)   As a driver, I agree that I will NOT engage in the following behaviors: texting while driving, social media while driving, shuffling playlist while driving. _____ (Initials)

4)   As a driver, I agree that I will not pick up or otherwise allow my cell phone to become a potential distraction while driving. _____ (Initials)

5)   As a driver, I agree to abide by the speed limit and recognize that exceeding the speed limit is unsafe and illegal. _____ (Initials)

6)   As a driver, I understand that driving after consuming alcohol or drugs makes me a less skilled driver and increases the likelihood that I will become involved in a crash. _____ (Initials)

7)   As a driver, I agree that I will not get behind the wheel of a motor vehicle if I have consumed any type of impairing substance. _____ (Initials)

8)   As a driver, I understand that my parents have the authority to suspend my driving privilege at any given time. _____ (Initials)

9)   As a driver, I understand that by violating any aspect of this agreement my parents may impose restrictions to include taking my license. _____ (Initials)

10) As a driver, I understand that poor decisions on my part could result in severe financial impacts on me and my family, including legal consequences such as fines, court costs, probation or even going to jail or prison. _____ (Initials)

11) As a driver, I recognize that poor decisions made on my part may result in injury or death to myself and others. _____ (Initials)

12) As a driver, I recognize that defensive driving is a choice, and I will make that choice every time I get behind the wheel. _____ (Initials)

_____

New Driver Signature

_____

Parent/Guardian Signature

_____

Date

ABOUT NCPP

The National Crash Prevention Program (NCPP) is a North Carolina based 501(c)(3) non-profit corporation dedicated to driver safety. An online defensive driving class featuring the authors can be found at nationalcpp. org. A portion of the proceeds from the video series and sales of this book are donated to other non-profit organizations with similarly aligned missions. If you would like to contact Joe and Ben to speak to your group, or if you would like to discuss ways to partner with NCPP to further its crime prevention mission, please visit our website today.

END NOTES

1. National Highway Traffic Safety Administration (NHTSA), *Distracted Driving Statistics*, www.nhtsa.gov.

2. Insurance Institute for Highway Safety (IIHS), *Speed and Fatality Facts*, www.iihs.org.

3. American Academy of Child & Adolescent Psychiatry, *Teen Brain Development and Decision Making*, www.aacap.org.

4. AAA Foundation for Traffic Safety, *Impact of Teen Passengers on Crash Risk*, www.aaafoundation.org.

5. Smith System Driver Improvement Institute, *Five Keys to Safe Driving*, www.smith-system.com.

6. Mothers Against Drunk Driving (MADD), *Statistics on Impaired Driving*, www.madd.org.

7. North Carolina General Statutes, Chapter 20: Motor Vehicles, including §20-138.1 (Impaired Driving) and §14-17 (Homicide).

8. Wilmington Police Department Crash Reconstruction Unit, Case Studies: *Alexandra's Crash*, *Thomas and the Cyclists*, and *Murder from Two Miles Away*.

9. NC Administrative Traffic Court Model – Developed by Ben David, DA for New Hanover & Pender Counties; now adopted statewide.

10. Federal Sentencing Guidelines for Drug Trafficking and Firearm Possession, U.S. Department of Justice.

11. "Acres of Diamonds" – Speech by Russell Conwell, Temple University, 1890.

12. Solomon Asch Conformity Experiment, 1951 – Published in *Scientific American*.

13. Maasai Tribal Culture – National Geographic, "Maasai: People of the Lion."

14. Defensive Driving Training Materials – Southeastern Driver Training Center, Wilmington, NC.

15. National Crash Prevention Program Video Series, www.nationalcpp.org.

www.ingramcontent.com/pod-product-compliance
Lightning Source LLC
Chambersburg PA
CBHW071311130626
46556CB00004B/1561